BRITAIN & SCOTLAND AND GERMANY

NEW HIGHER NHH HISTORY

BRITAIN & SCOTLAND AND GERMANY

John A. Kerr

James McGonigle

HODDER GIBSON

AN HACHETTE UK COMPANY

The front cover shows the flags of Scotland and Great Britain. The inset image shows the Statue of Victoria that sits on top of the Siegessaule (Victory Column) in Berlin. The monument celebrates the Prussian victory in the Danish–Prussian War.

The Publishers would like to thank the following for permission to reproduce copyright material:

Photo credits Source 1.1 Alamy/Mary Evans Picture Library; Source 1.2 Cartoonstock; Source 1.3 Alamy/Mary Evans Picture Library; Source 1.4 Alamy/Mary Evans Picture Library; Source 1.5 Cartoonstock; Source 1.6 Topfoto/HIP; Source 1.7 The Scotsman; Source 1.8 PA Photos/Dominic Lipinski; Source 1.9 Labour Representation Committee; Source 2.1 Topfoto/The Granger Collection; Source 2.2 Mary Evans Picture Library/The Women's Library; Source 2.3 Topfoto/Museum of London/HIP; Source 2.4 Mary Evans Picture Library/The Women's Library; Source 2.5 Orkney Archives; Source 2.6 Dundee City Council, Central Library; Source 2.7 Scotlandsimages.com, Crown Copyright 2009, The National Archives of Scotland, JC15/24/1; Source 2.8 Topfoto; Source 2.9 Alamy/David Riley; Source 2.10 Topfoto/Punch Ltd.; Source 3.1 Reproduced with permission from The Childrens Society; Source 3.2 Courtesy Oxford Classics; Source 3.3 Glasgow Caledonian University; Source 3.4 Topfoto/The Granger Collection; Source 3.5 Joseph Rowntree Foundation; Source 3.6 Bridgeman Art Library/Boer War Skirmish (gouache on paper), James Edwin McConnell (1903-95)/Private Collection/©Look and Learn; Source 3.7 Saturday Star/http://vne-resource.iol.co.za/51/picdb/lightbox_thumbs/c/9/109719; Source 3.8 Alamy/Mary Evans Picture Library/John Tennial; Source 4.1 Mary Evans Picture Library/Henry Grant; Source 4.2 Alamy/David Davis Photoproductions; Source 4.3 Punch; Source 4.4 Liberal Publication Department/Wikipedia; Source 4.5 Getty Images/Popperfoto; Source 5.1 Topfoto; Source 5.2 PA Photos; Source 5.3 Punch; Source 54.4 John Kerr; Source 5.5 Getty Images/Hulton Archive; Source 5.6 Image courtesy of Lothian Health Services Archive, Edinburgh University Library; Source 5.7 National Library of Wales/Solo Syndication/Associated Newspapers Ltd.; Source 5.8 Getty Images/Hulton Archive; Source 5.9 Douglas Corrance; Source 5.10 Topfoto; Source 5.11 Getty Images/Hulton Archive; Source 5.12 Corbis/Hulton Archive; Source 6.2 AKG images; Source 6.3 AKG Images; Source 6.4 Getty Images/Science & Society Picture Library; Source 7.1 Alamy/The Art Gallery Collection; Source 7.2 AKG Images; Source 7.3 Bridgeman Art Library/The Universal Social Republic, Allegory of the different peoples of Europe around the statue of the Rights of Man (colour litho), Frederic Sorrieu, (1807-c.1861)/Musee de la Ville de Paris, Musee Carnavalet, Paris, France/Archives Charmet; Source 7.4 AKG Images; Source 7.5 AKG Images; Source 8.1 AKG images; Source 9.1 AKG Images/Sotheby's; Source 9.2 AKG Images; Source 9.3 AKG Images; Source 9.4 BPK-Images.de; Source 9.6 AKG Images; Source 9.7 AKG Images/Ullstein Bild; Source 9.8 AKG Images; Source 9.9 Alamy/The Art Gallery Collection; Source 9.10 Corbis/Bettmann Archive; Source 10.2 AKG Images; Source 10.3 Corbis/Bettmann Archive; Source 10.4 AKG Images; Source 10.5 AKG Images; Source 10.6 Alamy/Interfoto; Source 10.10 Alamy/Mary Evans Picture Library; Source 11.2 Rex Features/Everett Collection; Source 11.3 KG Images; Source 11.4 Topfoto/The Granger Collection; Source 11.5 AKG Images; Source 11.6 Alamy/World History Archive; Source 11.8 Corbis/Michael Nicholson;

Every effort has been made to trace all copyright holders, but if any have been inadvertently overlooked the Publishers will be pleased to make the necessary arrangements at the first opportunity.

Index compiled by Indexing Specialists (UK) Ltd.

Although every effort has been made to ensure that website addresses are correct at time of going to press, Hodder Gibson cannot be held responsible for the content of any website mentioned in this book. It is sometimes possible to find a relocated web page by typing in the address of the home page for a website in the URL window of your browser.

Hachette's policy is to use papers that are natural, renewable and recyclable products and made from wood grown in sustainable forests. The logging and manufacturing processes are expected to conform to the environmental regulations of the country of origin.

Orders: please contact Bookpoint Ltd, 130 Milton Park, Abingdon, Oxon OX14 4SB. Telephone: (44) 01235 827720. Fax: (44) 01235 400454. Lines are open 9.00–5.00, Monday to Saturday, with a 24-hour message answering service. Visit our website at www.hoddereducation.co.uk. Hodder Gibson can be contacted direct on: Tel: 0141 848 1609; Fax: 0141 889 6315; email: hoddergibson@hodder.co.uk

© John A. Kerr and James McGonigle 2010
First published in 2010 by
Hodder Gibson, an imprint of Hodder Education,
An Hachette UK Company,
2a Christie Street
Paisley PA1 1NB

Impression number   5   4   3
Year   2013 2012 2011

Cover photo © Jon Arnold Images Ltd/Alamy (top), © Lance Bellers/iStockphoto (bottom), © les polders/Alamy (insert)
Illustrations by Jeff Edwards
Typeset in 11/14.5 pt Sabon by Pantek Arts, Maidstone, Kent
Printed in Italy

A catalogue record for this title is available from the British Library

ISBN-13: 978 0340 987 544

Contents

Introduction

What is in this book?

This book is for anyone studying two of the most popular topics in Paper 1 of the new Scottish Higher History course.

The first half of this book is about Britain from 1851 to 1951.

The second half is about Germany from 1815 to 1939.

Each topic in the new Higher History syllabus is divided into six issues.

Topic: **Later Modern History: Britain 1851–1951**
Issue 1 looks at the reasons why Britain became more democratic between 1867 and 1928.
Issue 2 asks in what ways Britain became more democratic between 1867 and 1928.
Issue 3 looks at the reasons why women in Britain gained greater political equality by 1928.
Issue 4 asks why the Liberal Government of the early twentieth century became involved in passing social reforms.
Issue 5 asks how effective were the Liberal Reforms in dealing with the problem of poverty in early twentieth-century Britain.
Issue 6 asks how well the Labour Government of 1945–1951 dealt with social problems facing Britain after the Second World War.

Topic: **Later Modern History: Germany 1815–1939**
Issue 1 looks at the most important reasons for the growth of nationalism in Germany between 1815 and 1850.
Issue 2 assesses how much German nationalism had grown by 1850.
Issue 3 considers how significant were the obstacles to German unification between 1815 and1850.
Issue 4 looks at how unification was achieved in Germany by 1871.
Issue 5 looks at how the Nazis achieved power in 1933.
Issue 6 considers what methods were most successful in keeping the Nazis in power between 1933 and 1939.

Why are there various activities throughout each chapter and at the end of each chapter?

Research in learning shows that if you just read as a means of learning, after 24 hours you will have retained about ten per cent of the new information. Unless learning is reinforced by action, it does not become anchored in either your short term or long term memory.

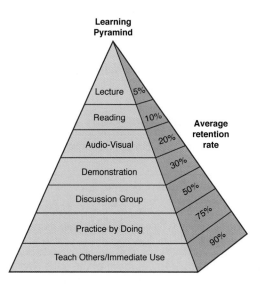

If an activity takes place soon after reading that requires you to use the information and process it in a different way than it was presented in the book, then your memory will retain over 60 per cent of the material. That is why each chapter has activities, the intention of which is to provide effective learning techniques to acquire and reinforce knowledge. Many of these activities can be applied to any topic with some slight adjustments. Some of the earlier activities try to establish good essay writing skills.

Each chapter also ends with typical exam essay questions, which will give you an idea of some of the ways the topic can be examined.

How to write a good essay

In Paper 1 you must write two essays, one from each of the two topics you have studied.

You will have 80 minutes to write the two essays.

That means you have a maximum of 40 minutes for each essay.

That does not leave much time for thinking.

You need to be prepared for the pressure of writing an essay in a fairly short time.

You will also have to write essays for your NABs and for your extended essay, so it's well worth knowing how to approach this aspect of the course.

There are **THREE** things you need to be able to do:

1 The first thing is to write in a well-structured way.

2 The second is to know enough factual information that is relevant to the question asked.

3 The third thing is to be able to USE your knowledge to write a relevant, direct answer to the question asked. Markers call this part of the answer your analysis.

How will my essays be marked?

Your essays are marked by giving a number of marks to each of the three stages outlined above. The first section is **structure**. That means your essay must have a clear beginning, middle and end. There are four marks available for this.

The second section is about **knowledge** and **understanding**. What relevant facts do you know about the topic of your essay? There are six marks available for this.

The third section is **analysis**. Marks will be given based on how well you **use** your knowledge to give an answer relevant to the question. There are ten marks available for this section.

The following grids will help you understand what should be in your essays and how they should be constructed. You should use these grids to help you to gain the best possible marks. Markers may use similar grids to help them decide what marks to award.

Structure (4 marks)	
0 marks	There is no attempt to organise your essay into an introduction, development or a conclusion.
1 mark	There is some attempt to provide a context. That means you describe events that are linked to the issue in the title.
	You try to develop your answer by writing relevant information about each of the main points in your introduction.
	You might have left out some main points from your answer.
	You might not have a conclusion clearly placed at the end of your essay. Instead, you might have a series of short answers to the main question throughout your answer.

2 marks	You have a clear introduction that sets the context.
	You do include several relevant points that you intend to develop in the essay.
	You include a lot of relevant information to explain the points raised in your introduction.
	Your information is organised into paragraphs.
	Each paragraph develops a separate main point.
	Your conclusion sums up the points you have made in answer to the main question.
3 marks	The introduction does the same as for two marks plus you make clear why you think your ideas are relevant to answering the main question.
	Your development is based on well-organised paragraphs, each one making a clear point in answer to the main question.
	Your conclusion sums up the ideas you have presented.
	You give a direct answer to the question supported by your evidence.
4 marks	Your introduction flows fluently and avoids just listing points.
	Your context shows a wide understanding of the background to the question.
	Your information is used to support an argument that deals closely with the question.
	Your conclusion is a balanced summary of the arguments made and reaches a conclusion which directly centres on the question.

Knowledge and Understanding

0–6 marks	You will score marks each time you use a correct and relevant piece of information to support a main point.
	You will get a second mark if you develop that information point further.
	However, you will not get a mark for every piece of information you include, even if it is factually correct and relevant. For example, an answer about Bismarck's role in German unification would not get six marks just for details about the Prussian wars. Such detail on the wars might only gain a maximum of two marks. You need to explain other aspects of Bismarck's role.
	Finally, you will not get any KU marks within your introduction so keep to the point. The introduction scores marks within the structure section.

Analysis

0–1 mark	You tend to use your information to tell a story.
	You make almost no attempt to answer the question.
2–3 marks	You still tend to tell a story BUT there are some recognisable attempts to answer the question.
4–5 marks	You use your information to answer the question although there might be some sections still in a story-telling style.
6–7 marks	You now make a consistent effort to use information to explain fully the ideas relevant to the question. Your information is in the essay for a purpose – not story telling.
8–10 marks	Your evidence is used consistently and thoroughly to examine the differing viewpoints based around the question before reaching a conclusion.
	You show you are aware that history is often about different points of view and you might even include some historiography.

BRITAIN & SCOTLAND

Contents

How and why did Britain become more democratic between 1867 and 1928?

In this chapter Issues 1 and 2 are combined. They deal with Britain's progress to democracy but while Issue 1 focuses on WHY the changes happened, Issue 2 deals with the evidence that shows HOW FAR Britain could be called democratic. Since the two issues have common factual content it makes sense to combine them in one chapter.

The first issue deals with the reasons why Britain became more democratic between 1867 and 1928. During this time, Britain underwent great social and political changes that resulted in it becoming more democratic. What were the motives for the changes in laws? Why should people who held political power be prepared to risk losing that power? Why was the right to vote (also known as 'the franchise') extended to more people? Was it pressure from campaigners, or did politicians see advantages for themselves or their party at a time of great social change? Changes in ideology, public and political attitudes and a developing economy were all ingredients in the recipe that caused change to happen.

The second issue is perhaps more straightforward. It asks for an assessment of how democratic Britain had become by 1928 compared to the middle of the nineteenth century. What had changed to make Britain more democratic? What are the main elements within a democracy? How far had they been achieved by 1928?

Why could Britain not be described as democratic in the early nineteenth century?

Throughout most of the nineteenth century there were two political parties called Conservative (Tory) and Liberal, but there was no such thing as a clear party policy or ideology. The political right to choose the government was granted to few men, and no women. Members of Parliament (MPs) were mainly interested in what they could get out of the system for themselves. Authority was in the hands of landowning wealthy men.

At the beginning of the nineteenth century many of Britain's landowners believed that not only was change undesirable, it also unnecessary. Such a view was expressed by Lord Braxfield during a trial of reform campaigners in Scotland in 1793:

> 'The British constitution is the best that ever was since the creation of the world, and it is not possible to make it better.'
>
> Lord Braxfield, 1793

But do not just assume that Braxfield and other members of the political establishment were selfish, or that the political system was deliberately unfair. The growth of democracy in Britain has a lot to do with changing ideas and attitudes about who should have political power.

Many students assume that those who supported the political system of the early to mid-nineteenth century were at best misguided or just wrong, but that assumption is to forget that attitudes and ideas change over time. There were people who argued for reform but those who opposed reform also believed firmly in their point of view. They believed that men who represented Britain represented the *land* of Britain, therefore who better to do that than the land owners? For example, read what was said in 1829 about the political system in Britain:

Source 1.1

According to the political cartoonist George Cruikshank, only political reform and the right to vote would lead to greater freedom and stop the destruction of civil rights.

> 'Britain is land. It is therefore the land owners – those who own the land of Britain – who deserve the right to govern. As long as the land lasts so does their commitment to sound government. The rabble? What right have they to vote? They own nothing of Britain and... cannot be trusted.'
>
> The Duke of Wellington, 1829

MPs today represent the people of Britain. Such an idea was alien to most politicians in the mid-nineteenth century who felt the mass of the people –

How and why did Britain become more democratic between 1867 and 1928?

the rabble, as some called them – could be ignored by the government as long as they caused no problems. The change in attitudes from parliament representing landowning interests to representing the people of the country was a major part in the move towards democracy.

Had the political system changed at all before 1867?

The first and very important step in changing the political system in Britain came with the 1832 Reform Act – often called the Great Reform Act. Until that time, little had changed for hundreds of years and although criticism of the unfairness and corruption within the system had been growing in the later eighteenth century, the outbreak of the French Revolution in 1789 turned the word 'reform' into something to be feared and opposed by those in authority. These people were concerned that reform would lead to revolution and therefore threaten their lives and property. To understand that reaction you must be aware that the French Revolution led directly to the murder of thousands of wealthy landowning aristocrats in France and even the execution of the King and Queen. Following the Revolution Britain was at war with France for 22 years.

By 1832 Britain was changing. The growing economy was producing a wealthy middle class who resented being excluded from the political system. They argued that, since they produced the wealth of Britain, they should have a say in its government. If they were ignored they could pose a threat but an alternative would be to absorb them into the system so that they would not challenge it.

Source 1.2

The bull at the bottom of the pyramid represents the bulk of the British population. How is it shown to be powerless? If it moved, the rest of society would collapse. Is the artist supporting or fearful of revolution?

Poor BULL & his Burden – or the Political MURRAIN !!!

Those who supported the Reform Bill of 1832 were not thinking about future progress towards democracy. Far from it! As you will see, many politicians saw reform as a way of taking the heat out of pressure for greater reform. They believed it was better to give some changes to defuse a situation than to block any change and risk a revolution. As historian and MP Thomas MacAuley said in 1831:

> 66 *I oppose universal suffrage because I think it would produce a destructive revolution...we say it is by property and intelligence that the nation ought to be governed.*
>
> Thomas MacAuley, 1831

However, he accepted that change was necessary:

> 66 *I support this [reform] because I am sure it is our best security against revolution...we must admit those it is safe to admit.*
>
> Thomas MacAuley, 1831

The point about 'admitting those it is safe to admit' is an important point to make when explaining why change happened, since it summarises an attitude to parliamentary reform that continued through the rest of the nineteenth century and into the twentieth – the point being that the vote, and political responsibility, could be given to 'respectable' groups who would not want to change the system too much but who, if they continued to be excluded, could be the focus of resentment, discontent and possibly revolution.

Did the Reform Act of 1832 make Britain more democratic?

The Reform Act changed the areas represented by MPs to reflect the population changes caused by industrialisation. The right to elect an MP (or sometimes two!) was taken away from some depopulated areas and the busier industrial towns got a few more MPs to represent them. Middle class males owning property of a certain value gained the vote but most people, including all women, had no political voice. Even after the reform the power of the aristocracy in government continued and at elections bribery and intimidation still existed. Five out of six males still could not vote and the distribution of MPs took little notice of the population moves of the previous 100 years, especially the demographic consequences of urbanisation. Women had no vote. Men with votes could still be intimidated or threatened. The House of Lords could still stop any change if it disapproved. MPs were still unpaid and to be an MP you had to own property. Britain was nowhere near being democratic in 1850.

Activities

1 Make a two column list.

In the first column list the reasons why Britain could not be called democratic before 1867.

The second column should list what had been done to make Britain more democratic before 1867. (The second column might not be very long!)

continued ➡

Activities *continued*

2 You are a radical reformer in the mid-nineteenth century. Prepare a pamphlet or news sheet to hand out in the street. You are taking a risk because the authorities may not like what you are doing. Your pamphlet should include certain things:

- Something to make people want to read it. You could try looking for images or cartoons of the time on the Internet.

- A short, witty headline making your point.

- A well laid-out article outlining why you want reform and what you want done to make Britain more democratic.

3 You are a Member of Parliament in the mid-nineteenth century. Prepare a speech lasting one minute explaining your concerns about the spread of leaflets and pamphlets in your area attacking the British system of government. In your speech, make clear what you think of reformers and why you think change is not necessary and, indeed, possibly dangerous to the country.

The Reform Act of 1867

The Reform Act gave the vote to every male adult householder living in a borough constituency. At that time, Britain was divided into borough and county constituencies. A constituency is an area of Britain in which the voters elect one MP and a borough constituency really meant a town or part of a city. By giving the vote to men owning property above a certain value and (male) lodgers paying rent above £10 a year, the vote was extended to skilled working men who could afford to live in property above that value. The effect of this reform nationally was to double the number of men who were entitled to vote and in the growing towns the increase was even greater – for example, the number of voters in Glasgow increased from 18,000 to 47,000.

The Reform Act also made representation in parliament fairer. Boroughs which had become depopulated lost their right to send MPs to parliament, while growing towns gained the right to send more. Fifteen towns that had never had an MP gained one, and an extra MP was given to Liverpool, Manchester, Birmingham and Leeds. Some counties which had increased in size also gained an MP.

This redistribution of MPs attempted to make political representation fairer – an important part of a democracy. However, the system was not yet fair with land-owning interests in the south of England still over-represented in parliament and the growing towns comparatively under-represented.

The 1867 Reform Act was a move towards greater democracy but, as most men and all women still had no vote and since voting was still open to bribery and intimidation, Britain remained a long way from democracy.

But why did a Conservative government pass a Reform Act in 1867 when it had opposed a Liberal Reform Act only a year before?

Historians see four main reasons to explain why the Second Reform Act became law in 1867. These are:

1   Social change creating pressure for political change

2   Changing political attitudes

3   Pressure from the people

4   Gaining a political advantage.

1   Social change creating pressure for political change

There were powerful forces in British society in the 1860s creating pressure for change and as future Liberal Prime Minister William Gladstone said in 1866:

> ❝ *'Time is on our side. The great social forces which move onwards in their might and majesty are on our side.'*

The industrial revolution changed where people lived, how they worked and how they felt about their position in society. It was a major contributor to greater urbanisation, demographic change (where people lived around Britain), the emergence of class structures and the decline in the power of landed aristocracy.

These social and economic changes created pressure to which politicians in the later nineteenth century had to respond.

The middle classes argued that since they were the wealth creators of the country they should have more of a say in the running of the country. Urbanisation also led to the rapid spread of ideas and emergence of class identity.

Source 1.3

One of the 'great social forces' was the growth of towns and cities. This cartoon from 1829 shows the army of the cities pushing back the countryside – urbanisation on the march.

LONDON going out of Town __ or __ The March of Bricks & Mortar.

The Industrial Revolution also demanded a more efficient transport network and the development of railways led to a national network of rapid and reliable communications. Railways, along with national newspapers, helped to create a national political identity where the people in Britain were aware of national issues. Newspaper owners saw the chance to widen their market and politicians were not slow to see the chance to spread their points of view far and wide. With the spread of basic education and the development of cheap new printing technology, popular newspapers aimed at the working classes spread national and local news. In response, political parties organised themselves into national units with local associations assisting the spread of national policies.

2 Changing political attitudes

Political attitudes were also changing and political reform was no longer seen as a threat. The new political ideologies of liberalism (the right of individuals to express their opinions freely) and democracy (the right of adults to choose the governments which ruled them) were becoming popular.

In the US and in Europe, struggles were taking place for liberty and a greater political say for 'the people'. Britain tended to support these moves elsewhere so how could the British government block these ideas in Britain? By the 1860s skilled working men in cities (called artisans) were more educated and respectable. They attended night schools, took part in local politics and were concerned with improving their living standards. Indeed, during the American Civil War (1862–65) many in Britain thought of the conflict in simple terms of a struggle between the modern 'democratic' Northern states, who wanted to free black slaves, and the old fashioned South, which fought to retain slavery. As a sign of support for the 'North' and to put some economic pressure on the 'South' some British textile workers even chose to accept wage cuts rather than work with cotton picked by slaves in the US.

Such actions and arguments convinced some politicians that the artisan class were respectable and responsible members of society with 'a moral conscience' and deserved the right to vote.

3 Pressure from the people

It is also claimed that politicians were pushed towards reform by pressure groups. It is true that groups such as the Reform Union and the Reform League, and demonstrations of 100,000 in Glasgow, certainly helped to persuade politicians of the need to consider reform. Historian Royden Harrison combined the growing respectability of the artisans with fear of disturbances and even revolution when he explained why reform happened. He believed that the working classes had reached a point where it was safe to grant the right to vote but it was dangerous not to do so. He believed a revolutionary spirit existed in 1860s Britain, created by a trade depression that spread unemployment and a cholera epidemic that spread fear. He also argued that the Hyde Park riots of July 1866 and the Reform League's campaigns all pressurised parliament to make changes.

However, later historians reject that idea, arguing there is no evidence that parliament was pressured to reform by external groups. In fact, the Reform Act of 1867 created changes which went beyond what leaders of the reform groups wanted. So if social forces were only influential in persuading politicians of the need for reform, what were the more immediate, more practical reasons for the real cause of reform?

1

How and why did Britain become more democratic between 1867 and 1928?

Source 1.4

Demonstrations organised by trade unionists and the Reform League between 1866 and 1867 in support of an extension of the franchise to working men played a major part in the passing of the Second Reform Act in 1867.

4 Gaining a political advantage

In 1867, the Conservative Party became the government after twenty years out of power. Was the Reform Act therefore the result of cynical opportunism by the Conservatives trying to maintain their hold on power, or was it a genuine attempt to spread democracy in Britain?

There were immediate political advantages to be gained from the Reform Act in 1867. What created the real chance of change was Lord Palmerston's death in October 1865. As Liberal Prime Minister, Palmerston had blocked any suggestions of reform for a long time, but after his death a new proposal for reform split the Liberals between those who wanted reform and those who did not. This was the Conservatives' opportunity. If the Conservatives continued to do nothing it was likely the Liberals would win the next election and the Conservatives would face more years out of power.

Historians refer to the Conservative Reform Act of 1867 as 'dishing the Whigs' by 'stealing the Liberal's clothes'. What does that mean? Quite simply, Benjamin Disraeli, the leader of the Conservative Party in the House

of Commons, believed that if his party gave the vote to working class men in the towns then those men were likely to vote Conservative in future! So in 1867 the Conservative Party stole many of the Liberals' ideas about political reform ('stole their clothes') and spoiled their chances of winning support from working class men. An old fashioned word for spoiling something is 'to dish it' and an old name for the Liberals was 'Whig' – so that is why 'dish the Whigs' is used when referring to 1867 Reform Act.

A 'Leap in the Dark'?

This phrase was used by Prime Minister Lord Derby when the Reform Act was passed. It means a risky move into an unknown area. But was the Reform Act really such a political risk?

Source 1.5

Disraeli, on the winning horse, with Gladstone close behind. They were both in the race to be the first to pass a parliamentary reform act in the late 1860s.

THE DERBY, 1867. DIZZY WINS WITH "REFORM BILL."

Mr. PUNCH. "*Don't be too sure; wait till he's* WEIGHED."

By winning favour with the electorate, the Conservatives were running no risk of really losing any power. Although the number of voters in boroughs (towns) was increased, the candidates they voted for were almost entirely members of the property-owning classes. The two parties they could vote for – Conservative and Liberal – also represented stability and old values, so the control of government was still in the hands of the wealthy elite. Traditional influences would continue to ensure control by the established social order, so reform was no real threat to the system. Rather, it removed pressure from reformist pressure groups, responded to the social changes of the time and established the Conservative Party as a party of government.

Given their immediate political needs, the opportunity that opened up in 1867, and their possession of an outlook which allowed them to hope that Reform would be 'safe', one can understand why the Conservatives came to pass the Reform Act of 1867.

Source 1.6

As Britain seems to hide its face from possible danger, Disraeli's face on the horse leaps bravely into the bushes marked 'reform'. Other politicians hang back, seemingly worried about where reform might lead. But was it really a risk?

A LEAP IN THE DARK.

Activities

This section has identified four main reasons why the 1867 Reform Act was passed.

Work with a partner.

- Leave a space for a title for this work.

- Divide a page of your workbook into four columns.

- At the top of each column, write a sub heading making clear one of the four reasons for passing the 1867 Reform Act.

- Agree on no more than three sentences to summarise each of the reasons why the reform act was passed.

- Use colour to differentiate the four reasons.

Explain why it would be correct to say the 1867 Reform Act made Britain *more* democratic, but wrong to say it made Britain democratic.

Agree on a clear, short, relevant and memorable title for this activity and write it larger than the rest of your writing. Use a different colour to make your title stand out.

Increasing democracy between 1867 and 1885

Between 1867 and 1885 more reforms took Britain further along the road towards democracy.

Apart from increasing the number of voters, reform also involved making elections less corrupt and the process of voting fair and free from bribery and intimidation. The redistribution of parliamentary seats to ensure MPs represented roughly equal numbers of people was also part of increasing democracy.

Greater fairness at elections

Corruption was a serious problem in British politics even after the 1867 Reform Act. Despite increasing the electorate from eight per cent of adults to 28 per cent, the newly enfranchised men found their freedom restricted by the system of open voting and by the excessive spending activities of wealthy candidates at election.

Before 1872, voters cast their votes publicly and this could clearly lead to intimidation, threats and loss of homes and jobs if the voter did not support the choice of his employer. For example, in Bradford, in England, voters working in woollen mills overwhelmingly supported the mill owner's preferred choice of candidate. Candidates eager to 'buy' votes could offer food and drink and even jobs to likely voters. The Secret Ballot Act of 1872 allowed voters to vote in secret in polling booths and that certainly helped remove the more obvious examples of intimidation and bribery.

The Corrupt and Illegal Practices Act 1883

Spending on elections by the big parties rose to huge sums but in 1883 the Corrupt and Illegal Practices Act limited how much candidates could spend during election time. It banned such activities as the buying of food or drink for voters. A detailed list of illegal and corrupt election practices was created and candidates had to account for all election expenses. The law even stated how many carriages could be used by political parties carrying voters to the polls.

Redistribution of Seats

In 1867 and again in 1885, laws were passed to try to reflect more accurately the changing population pattern of Britain. The laws tried to make each MP represent roughly the same number of people. In 1885, 79 towns, whose populations had fallen, lost their right to elect an MP. Another 36 towns with falling populations had the number of MPs representing them reduced to one each. At the same time, growing towns were given the right to elect 2 MPs and even larger towns were divided into several constituencies, each one electing an MP.

The Third Reform Act, 1884

The power of the land-owning aristocracy of Britain was declining but they had prevented the 1867 Act from going further and giving the vote to country workers. The old rural elite resented the increasing power of the middle and working classes and while the Liberals argued that people living in towns and rural areas should have equal rights, the Conservatives resisted such ideas. However, in 1884 Prime Minister William Gladstone proposed further parliamentary reform which would give working class men in the countryside the same voting rights as those living in the towns. As he said:

> *Is there any doubt that the people living in the countryside are capable citizens, qualified for the vote and able to make good use of their power as voter?*
>
> *William Gladstone, 1884*

Had the reforms really made Britain more democratic?

The practical effects of the reforms were obvious. The Third Reform Act increased the electorate by 50 per cent. The process of voting became peaceful and orderly. Whereas in some constituencies before 1872 over 400 police were needed to keep order, newspapers reported that since the ballot had been passed there had been no trouble at any election.

However, the more important question as to whether or not the reforms made Britain a much more democratic society remains unclear.

Joseph Chamberlain called the Third Reform Act 'the greatest revolution this country has ever undergone' and foresaw 'government of the people by the people'. But was it?

If such an opinion was true, why then did later historians comment, 'the reforms were a dazzling display of change' covering up 'continuity of background attitudes'? As D.G. Wright wrote:

> *By modern standards, Victorian democracy was undemocratic. Although the democratic principle was accepted in 1867, one man, one-vote never existed in Victorian Britain, even after the Third Reform Act.*
>
> *D.G. Wright, Democracy and Reform 1815–1885, 1970*

The reforms of 1867 and 1885 had immediate effects on the process of voting and representation in parliament but in terms of their impact on moving towards 'people power', little changed. Perhaps that was the intention.

After the reforms, the system favoured a party with resources and the ability to organise efficiently those entitled to vote, while old traditional interests still influenced an electorate accustomed to 'acknowledging their betters'. In Blackburn, one MP continued unchallenged for 24 years. Could it be because of his party's donations to local football clubs, churches and other organisations?

Even voting was not made completely fair. One undemocratic feature of nineteenth-century voting, which continued into the twentieth century, was plural voting. Men who owned property in a constituency different from the one in which they lived gained an extra vote (or more, depending on the businesses they owned) while university graduates had a vote in both their home and university constituencies.

Why were the political reforms of the later nineteenth century passed?

Once again, there are several reasons suggested why parliament passed the reforms, but do they stand up to close examination?

Popular pressure

A traditional argument is that the Third Reform Act was the result of popular pressure. In reality such pressure was not significant.

It is true that before the 1832 and 1867 Reform Acts large-scale organised demonstrations in support of change united middle and working class reform supporters. However, before the Third Reform Act in 1884 there was little widespread popular pressure. Some pressure came from Trade Unions, the Reform League and the Reform Union and on 21 July 1884 a franchise demonstration procession took three hours to pass Parliament. However, this demonstration was not typical of the time and few thought it merited the description of 'intimidation Monday'. By the 1880s the political situation was very different from the 1830s and reform campaigners used contacts within parliament and within political parties to pursue their cause. In short, popular pressure had little effect on governments that had their own motives for reform.

Political advantage

Parliamentary reform was the result of new legislation passed by parliament. In other words, reform was not forced upon parliament but was granted by it and it can be argued that the hope of gaining a political advantage was at the heart of much of the change.

The political party most associated with the reforms of the later nineteenth century was the Liberal Party, which was a mixture of reformist groups and many who resented the power of the old land-owning aristocracy. For example, pressure for a secret ballot came from reformist John Bright within the cabinet. Bright, along with other Radicals (activists who wanted major social and political change in Britain) believed that the increasing working class electorate would use their 'political voice' to promote social reforms – but only if they were free from worry about their homes and jobs. They would need to be able to vote in secret, free from retaliation by their bosses and landlords who might not agree with their choice.

Even the Corrupt and Illegal Practices Act of 1883 can be seen as a pragmatic, practical move by the Liberals. By limiting the amount of spending on elections, some Liberals believed the advantage held by wealthier Conservative opponents would be reduced. This made political reform an action based on the hope that reform would give an advantage to the party in power.

The argument that democracy spread because of a significant change in ideas and attitudes is also questionable and rather simplistic. One illustration of the argument that change had much more pragmatic reasons came in the 'Arlington Street Compact' by which Gladstone, the Liberal leader and Prime Minister, met with Salisbury, the Conservative leader, to 'do a deal' over the Third Reform Act. To soothe Conservative worries over his proposals for reform, Gladstone promised another reform to redistribute the constituencies of Britain. The effect of redistribution created many 'safe' Conservative parliamentary seats in the growing suburbs of cities. Reassured that Conservative strength would not be hurt by the Third Reform Act, Salisbury agreed to accept the Liberal proposals.

To underline the argument of advantage, the big political reforms of the Liberal government of the 1880s could be considered a distraction from major overseas problems. Also, by placing the reforms close to the next election, the Liberals hoped to gain advantage from grateful new voters in towns more fairly represented after the redistribution of seats. Overall, when considering political reform it is more realistic to see politicians moving their attitudes to accommodate changes that, in the long run, they suspected were unavoidable. At the same time they tried to ensure that their own party's political interests would be protected in times of change. It could therefore be argued that party leaders created the reforms mainly to promote their own party's political interests. Clearly the political leaders of Britain trusted and controlled the reform process. Reform was not the result of fear of pressure groups forcing change.

Were there other social and economic developments pushing Britain towards democracy?

To judge whether or not a state is democratic, it is never enough to simply count the number of voters. The growth of democracy cannot be described or explained simply by listing new laws which extended the franchise. Other developments provide foundations on which to build a democratic society.

The development of elementary (or primary) education for all in the 1870s provided a literate society who could read the increasing number of newspapers.

The growth of public libraries and the spread of the railways also provided greater access to information. The railways reduced the isolation of some parts of the country and helped develop a national political consciousness.

By the 1880s, the British population were well informed about national political issues and were greedy to see the political celebrities of the day. Modern-day disillusion with politics had not set in and when Prime Minister William Gladstone used the railways for tours around Midlothian,

Source 1.7

New public libraries, such as the Central Library in Edinburgh, provided information and a place for discussion – vital in a democratic society.

thousands of people from neighbouring towns and villages came to hear him speak. It was reported that there were 50,000 people for only 6000 seats. On the other hand, older, more 'traditional' politicians complained, 'This dirty business of making political speeches is an aggravation we owe entirely to Mr Gladstone.' However, the point was made. The public were informed and now saw themselves as part of the political process.

The idea of democracy in Britain had become well rooted by the later nineteenth century, but further change was necessary. Electors had little choice, women had no right to vote and the power of the House of Lords was still unrestricted. Perhaps Joseph Chamberlain was rather premature when he described political change at the end of the nineteenth century as 'a revolution which has been peacefully and silently accomplished. The centre of power has been shifted.' Nevertheless, by 1900 Britain had become much more democratic than it had been in 1850.

Activities

This is similar to the earlier tasks about 1850. By repeating all or some of the tasks you will be able to see what progress Britain had made towards democracy in the 50 years since 1850.

1   Make a two column list.

   The first column should list reasons why Britain could not be called fully democratic in 1900.

   The second column should list what had been done to make Britain more democratic by 1900.

   Think of appropriate headings for your two columns.

2   You are a political reformer at the start of the twentieth century. Prepare a newspaper article outlining why Britain was not yet a democracy and what should be done to make it more of a democracy. Your article should:

   • make people want to read it

   • contain a short witty headline making your point

   • contain your main objections to the present system

   • make detailed suggestions for further reform

   • be concise and no bigger than one A4 page.

3   You are a Member of Parliament in 1900. Prepare a speech lasting one minute explaining your concerns about the spread of newspaper articles attacking the British system of government. In your speech, make clear what you think of proposals for change and why you think they are not necessary.

Greater democracy after 1900

After 1900, issues concerning the spread of democracy focussed on three main areas. The first was restricting the power of the unelected House of Lords. The second was to allow the participation of all men in the political process, not just voting. Finally, there was the issue of votes for women.

Reforming the House of Lords

In 1900 members of the House of Lords were not elected yet they had power to veto, or block, any of the proposals for new laws (Bills) made by the elected House of Commons. The power of the unelected House of Lords over the elected House of Commons was a direct challenge to any suggestion that Britain was a democratic state.

Although proposals to reform the House of Lords had been made in the later nineteenth century and again in the early 1900s, nothing had come of them. The Lords had even blocked reform proposals to increase democracy such as plans to abolish plural voting.

The catalyst for change came when the Liberal Government wanted to pass a series of social reforms. These reforms would cost money so the government planned to raise taxes by means of a Budget (officially called a Money Bill). The 1909 Budget was nicknamed 'The Peoples Budget' in view of the social reforms to be paid for partly by increased taxation.

Source 1.8

Until 1911, the House of Lords had a power of veto over the House of Commons. The unelected Lords could prevent any bill they disliked from becoming law.

The Government proposed to raise taxation on motor tax, alcohol and a super tax on the very wealthy. The wealthy upper classes did not like it but since the Liberals were the government there seemed little that could be done to stop it. However, the House of Lords had the power to veto any suggestion for a new law made by the House of Commons and that is what they did. The Conservatives, who had a large majority in the House of Lords, objected to this attempt to 'tax the rich to help the poor' and declared that they intended to veto the People's Budget. If the budget did not become law, the Liberals could not raise taxes and so could not pay for the social reforms.

The issue of democracy and 'who rules the country' was on everyone's lips.

The Liberals reacted by making speeches in working class areas on behalf of their reforms and portraying the Lords as men who were using their privileged position to stop the poor from getting a better life. The result was that the House of Lords became extremely unpopular with the British people and the Liberal Government decided to take action to reduce its powers.

The conflict between 'peers and people' is essential to the growth of democracy in Britain. Since the elected government of Britain had decided to pass a new law (the budget is a type of law called a Money Bill), what right did the non-elected House of Lords have to stop it? After a long argument and two more elections, the Parliament Act of 1911 resolved the situation. The Act was an important step on the road to democracy in Britain. It reduced the power of the House of Lords so that they had no say over budgets and could no longer veto bills passed by the House of Commons. They could only delay them for two years.

The Parliament Act also reduced the maximum length of time between general elections from seven years to five and provided payment for Members of Parliament, thereby allowing men of the working class to consider standing for election as an MP.

Participation – the opportunity to become an MP

The opportunity to participate fully in the electoral process is an essential ingredient in the democracy recipe.

For most of the nineteenth century, MPs were not paid and had to own land. Although the property qualification to become an MP ended in the 1850s, working class men, who had to work for their living for fairly low wages, could not afford to give up their day jobs to become 'a politician'. For Britain to be a democracy, the chance to become an MP would have to be opened to everyone. In 1911, MPs began to be paid, thereby allowing ordinary people to participate more fully in the political process.

Increasing choice

After the Third Reform Act in 1884, there was no national working class party to attract the votes of the newly enfranchised working class men.

Instead, these men tended to vote for the Liberals and a pattern of working class support for the Liberals was established. In the 1880s, working class political representatives stood in parliamentary elections as Liberal-Labour candidates and after the 1885 General Election there were eleven of these Lib-Lab MPs. However, socialists and others within the Labour movement began to argue that the working classes needed their own independent political party.

Indeed, working class men who were elected as MPs (often sponsored by their trade union) were called Lib-Lab members. The development of the Labour Party is most easily explained as a series of alliances between socialist groups and the realisation by trade unions that it would be helpful to have a political voice in parliament. It was the trade unions that agreed to finance the Labour Party with money from the subscriptions paid by union members. As a result, the Labour Representation Committee (LRC) (soon called the Labour Party) was formed.

Source 1.9

By 1900, the LRC was providing a choice for working class voters.

This was an important development in British democracy because without a party to express the wishes of sections of the electorate, what genuine voice did they have in the government of the country? Not all the working classes voted Labour, of course. But the creation of the Labour Party provided choice, an essential ingredient in a democratic society.

The effect of the Great War, the Reform Act of 1918 and votes for women

The 1918 Representation of the People Act gave all men over the age of 21 the right to vote (and those aged 19, if they had been on active service in the armed forces). It also gave the vote to women over the age of 30 who were householders, the wives of householders, occupiers of property with an annual rent of £5 or graduates of British universities. The electorate increased to about 21 million, of which 8.4 million were women – about 40 per cent of the total voters. The reasons given for this change are always linked to the effect of the Great War.

Votes for women

In August 1914, the campaign for votes for women came to an end. It was felt unpatriotic to continue causing problems for the government while the country was at war.

It is true that women's war work was important to Britain's eventual victory, but has the importance of the Great War to the cause of women's suffrage been exaggerated? Did votes for women remain a 'live' issue during the war, or did other factors move the government towards votes for women in 1918?

One traditional explanation for the granting of the vote to some women in 1918 has been that women's valuable work for the war effort radically changed male ideas about their role in society and that giving them the vote in 1918 was almost a 'thank you' for their efforts. But remember that the women who worked long hours and risked their lives in munitions factories were mostly single and in their late teens or early twenties. The women who were given the vote were 'respectable' ladies, aged 30 or over who were property owners or married to property owners.

Perhaps, once again, gaining political advantage is a better explanation. The Russian Revolution had made governments across Europe worried of any social disorder. During the war many women had become aware of their own influence and ability to make changes to improve their living and working conditions. Could the government be sure that these women would not join a revitalised Suffragette campaign after the war and return to Suffragette 'terrorism'?

The government was also aware that changes in the law about male voters were necessary. Politicians grew anxious to enfranchise more men, many of whom had lost their qualification to vote as a result of moving home for war service. It was politically unacceptable to tell those soldiers returning from the war that they had lost their right to vote, so the rules had to change. The issue of conscription had also forced a rethink of the relationship between male citizens of the UK and their government. In 1916, men were ordered to join the armed forces or do work of national importance. Was it right that the government could order men to fight and kill on its behalf and not allow these men a chance to choose the government? That is why when the election was finally held in 1919, all men who had been in the armed forces were allowed to vote at 19 – they did not have to wait until 21.

The creation of a wartime coalition also opened the door to change. Prime Minister Asquith, an opponent of women's suffrage, was replaced by the more pragmatic David Lloyd George. His support for the enfranchisement of some women undoubtedly made change easier to accomplish. But those arguments may reveal too negative an attitude towards the women's

1

How and why did Britain become more democratic between 1867 and 1928?

campaign and their wartime efforts. Undoubtedly, the sight of women 'doing their bit' for the war effort gained them some respect and balanced the negative publicity of the earlier Suffragette campaign. The actions of women during the war even converted earlier opponents, including Asquith.

The vote at last

At the time, the 1918 Representation of the People Act seemed a major victory for the Suffragist movement. However, politically, women were still not the equal to men in Britain – men could vote on an age qualification alone and nine years before women, who still had to 'qualify'. Even then, about 22 per cent of women of 30 years of age and above were denied the right to vote as they were not property owners.

Activities

This activity is to help you organise information and prepare for writing an essay. Allow one A4 page.

Design a spider diagram. The first stage of the diagram up to the names at the ends of the legs should fill only a small section in the middle.

The body of the spider should have a question written on it – How far did Britain become more democratic between the mid-nineteenth century and 1928?

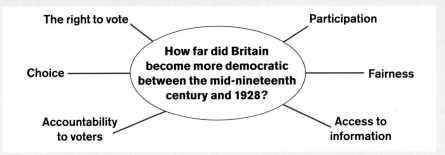

Your spider only has six legs coming from it. At the end of each leg write one of the following words or phrases clearly: The right to vote; Fairness; Choice; Access to information; Accountability to voters; Participation (which means the right to take part in the political system).

Colour (do NOT highlight) each of your phrases differently.

From each new word or phrase, draw another short leg and then beside it list all the detailed information you can find to explain how each of these words or phrases were achieved.

When done, gently shade all your details the same colour as the colour you used for the main word or phrase.

You now have an organised collection of information ready to use – and you have used one technique for creating useful and organised notes.

Essay Writing

This activity shows you how to plan an essay based on the question:

> **Why was the right to vote given to more and more people between 1867 and 1918?**

First of all, read the earlier pages about essay writing in this book carefully. You will see that you gain marks for three sections of your essay – structure, development and analysis.

Your structure must start with an introduction. You will also read about why different marks are given for structure.

What is the difference between a poor introduction and a good one?

To answer that question it is best to use some real examples.

Here is a very weak introduction to the question asked in this activity:

In order to answer this question it is necessary to explain why more people got the vote between 1867 and 1918. Lots of reforms were passed to give the vote to more people and there were lots of reasons why this happened.

Why is this a very weak introduction?

- It is far too short – only two sentences long.
- This introduction does nothing to help the writer. Time is wasted by almost writing out the question. All it does is pretend to be an introduction.
- There is no thought here about how the essay will develop.
- There is no signposting of any ideas about why the reforms happened.

Here is a much better introduction:

There were many reasons why the franchise was extended to more and more people between 1867 and 1918. These reasons included avoiding possible revolution (1), trying to win advantages for a particular political party (2), pressure from various groups (3) and the effect of the Great War (4), which acted as a catalyst and speeded up change. Another important reason for change was the effect of the Industrial Revolution (5), which changed where people lived, how they worked and how they felt about their position in society. Finally, another important reason why the franchise was extended was the change in political ideology which changed (6) from believing the right to vote should only belong to people who owned the land of Britain to believing that the vote should be the right of all adult British citizens.

continued ➡

Essay Writing *continued*

Why is this a better introduction?

- It is an appropriate length. The style is mature and signposts clearly the points to be raised in the essay. If it helps, there is no reason why you cannot faintly number your separate points with a pencil (as in the example), as a guide to yourself for what the main development paragraphs should be about.
- It provides a structure which the candidate can follow through the rest of the exam.
- There is no irrelevance and it is clear to a marker the candidate has understood the question.

After the introduction your tasks are as follows:

- Find as many relevant facts as you can. You will include these as development of your first point, where you show off your knowledge of how the right to vote was gained by more people, thereby making Britain more democratic.

- Follow through this process to acquire information relevant for all of the numbered sections in your introduction. When that is complete, you know you have developed all the points in your introduction and all that remains to do is write a conclusion which answers the main question.

Now here is an example of how to develop the points made in your introduction. In other words, to see the sort of information you would be expected to include in each paragraph to develop them suitably. The numbers refer to the numbers in the sample introduction:

(1) This point sets the context, establishes that the candidate knows what the question is about and shows knowledge of when the reform acts were passed. It also lets the marker know that the candidate intends to deal with why the reforms happened (which is what the question asks) rather than write down the terms of the act which is seldom asked about directly.

(2) This is a reference to political parties adopting the ideas of other parties and attracting voters by promising changes in order to prevent the other party from winning an election. That was especially true of the circumstances around the 1867 Reform Act. The phrases 'stealing the Liberals clothes' and 'dishing the Whigs' would be appropriate here if you know what they mean!

continued ➡

Essay Writing *continued*

(3) Here the point should be made that by 1867 urban skilled working class men were educated and not revolutionary – so why not admit them to the political system by granting them the vote? In 1884 the same was true of other men in the countryside and in towns. If they were not admitted, they might turn to the new ideology of socialism which was seen as a threat. There were also views that working people were citizens of the country and deserved to have a vote as the ideology of democracy gained greater acceptance in the country. Another more cynical point could be that the ordinary electorate could only vote and had no political influence within parliament. They were far from the reigns of power, which were still in the hands of the educated and wealthy elite within parliament.

(4) The Great War changed many attitudes. Most answers state that women gained the vote because of their war work. That is not entirely true. Most of the women who worked in the war effort were below 30, so they got no vote in 1918. Perhaps there were other reasons for extending the franchise in 1918. One clue could be that for one election only, right after the war, ex-servicemen who were 19 or over gained the vote. So perhaps changes in the right to vote had more to do with the conscription of young men to fight and the realisation that, as citizens, people had the right to choose a government which may decide to send off men to kill on behalf of that government? So maybe this point about the effect of the Great War is not as simple as was first thought. After all, this reform extended the vote to all MEN over 21 as well as women over 30. But the war was certainly a catalyst for change.

(5) This is an important point to make. Britain was changing very fast after 1850. Cities were growing and social classes were emerging. Large cities and factories housed thousands of people who suffered terrible working and living conditions. If they were not taken 'into' the system by giving them the vote, would they try to overthrow the system with revolution? It was also true that other industrial countries were becoming more democratic. Political 'freedom' issues had become popular in the USA and Europe in the later nineteenth century. Why not in Britain also?

(6) A main theme in this course is change in ideology. By 1918 there was a belief that parliament represented the people of Britain, not just the owners of land and property. A point to make could be that by 1918 the vote was considered to be a right for the many and not a privilege for the few.

continued ➡

Essay Writing *continued*

The Conclusion

Here is a guide to writing the conclusion for the question 'Why was the vote given to more and more people between 1867 and 1918?'

● Start by writing 'In conclusion…' and write one sentence that makes a general answer to the main question.

● Then write 'On one hand…' and summarise your information that supports one point of view about the main question.

● Then write 'On the other hand…' and here you must sum up the evidence that gives a different point of view about the main question.

● Finally write 'Overall…' and then write an overall answer to the main question, perhaps including the most important point that led you to your final overall answer.

Here is an example conclusion:

In conclusion there was no single reason to explain why more people gained the vote. On one hand long term changes in population and society led to growing demands for the vote for middle class men and then for working class men and women. On the other hand single events such as the Great War also created the right circumstances for change. Overall, however, the most common reason for change was that the political parties saw some advantage for themselves in extending the franchise. After all, why grant reforms that would disadvantage the party in power?

Sample Essay Questions

Other essay types in this section could be:

1 How far was Britain a democracy by 1918?

2 Economic changes in Britain led to political changes. How far can that view of the reasons for franchise reform be supported between 1867 and 1918?

3 'By 1914 Britain was not yet a democratic country'. How valid is that view?

2 Why did women gain the right to vote?

The campaigns for women's rights, and in particular women's suffrage, must be seen within the context of changing society and the huge social and political changes happening in Britain in the late nineteenth and early twentieth centuries. A starting point to understand both the campaigns of women and the position of men is to look at attitudes about the sexes and how these changed between the 1850s and 1928, when all women gained political equality with men.

Source 2.1

Votes for women!

Different Spheres

A generally held view is that women in the later nineteenth century were considered to be 'second class citizens' – physically, mentally and morally inferior to men and therefore incapable of voting. However, a more appropriate description of mid-nineteenth century attitudes towards women is that women were considered to be not only physically different, but also emotionally and mentally. It was argued that women and men operated in different 'spheres', with their social roles being based on their differing abilities. While men were the protectors of family and the 'breadwinners' who had a role to play in government and professional life, women, by contrast, should be focused on rearing the children and doing 'good deeds' in charitable religious and educational work. As was said in a parliamentary debate in 1872, 'We regard women as something to admire, to love...she is the silver lining which lights the cloud of man's existence'. A comment by Sarah Sewell, herself opposed to women's suffrage, is often used to represent the stereotype of wife and mother:

> 66 *The profoundly [well] educated women rarely make good wives or mothers…[they] seldom have much knowledge of pies and puddings… nor do they enjoy the interesting work of attending to small children.*
>
> Sarah Sewell

It was also argued that 'political' women would neglect their female duties and lose their femininity. Women were said to be too emotionally unstable for rational thought and were clearly unsuited to serious matters, fit only for 'women's work'. On top of these accusations of inferiority, Queen Victoria simply fed anti-feminist prejudices by describing the women's suffrage campaign as 'that mad wicked folly of women's rights'.

In law, it also seemed at first sight that women really were treated as second class citizens. In the mid-nineteenth century, when a woman married (and was 'given away' by one man to another) all her possessions became her husband's property, including clothes and any money she earned. Women had no legal rights over their children and husbands could legally imprison their wives and beat them with a stick.

Source 2.2

This cartoon shows a scene only too familiar to many women in the later nineteenth century. And today?
It was hoped that with the vote women could gain better rights.

Women who spoke out against this were answered by claims that they were already well represented in parliament, the courts and the world in general by their fathers, brothers and husbands. But change was happening and it would be wrong to assume that these descriptions of women as dependent, 'second class citizens' held true for all women up until 1918. Quite simply, that assumption is wrong.

Changing society

Social change was an important factor in creating an atmosphere of acceptance in terms of women's suffrage. Millicent Fawcett, a leader of the National Union of Women's Suffrage Societies (NUWSS), had argued that wider social changes were vital factors in winning the right to vote. Her argument was supported in a parliamentary debate in 1912.

> 66 *[Arguments against giving women the vote] are both out of date and out of place. They might have been correct and proper two or three centuries ago...but not in the twentieth century, when women have for years, by common consent, taken an active part in public affairs, when they are members of town councils, boards of guardians and... are prominent members of political associations...*
>
> Millicent Fawcett, parliamentary debate, 1912

As early as 1793, in *A Vindication of the Rights of Women*, Mary Wollstonecraft argued that women were deliberately moulded as superficial, rather silly creatures, maintained in a childlike dependency on men and it was not until several laws were passed between 1873 and 1893 that the social position of women improved. The Infant Custody Act gave mothers increased rights over their children, even to the extent of allowing some mothers custody of their children after conviction for adultery. The Married

Source 2.3

Attitudes were changing by 1900. This poster tries to show the unfairness of denying women the right to vote – although some of its comparisons are not politically correct today.

Women's Property Acts of 1882 and 1893 granted women full legal control of all property they had owned at marriage or that they had gained after marriage by their own earnings or through inheritance. The education of women also improved with universal primary education for boys and girls from the 1870s and at the other end of the scale universities increasingly opened their doors to both men and women. Women began to enter 'white collar' office jobs as well as the more traditional jobs of teaching and nursing. Of course, the 'marriage bar' still applied, which meant that women usually had to leave their jobs when they married.

Politically, the status of some women also changed with the Local Government Act of 1894, which granted women ratepayers and property occupiers the right to vote in local elections and the opportunity to stand for election. Women also became involved in political activity, joining political parties, working as volunteers organising social events, canvassing voters and making speeches. However, as was pointed out by Harold Baker MP speaking in 1912:

> *The exact numbers of women who were serving in public capacities [was very small]…on town councils there were only 24 women out of a total of 11,140…and on county councils there were only 4 women out of a total of 4,615.*
>
> Harold Baker, 1912

Nevertheless, doors had been opened.

The overall effect of these developments was to erode male prejudices. Attitudes that were once widespread were, by the end of the century, changing. In effect, the stereotyped views of women outlined earlier were seen as old fashioned

Source 2.4

The 'John' in this cartoon refers to John Bull, a figure representing the British government. In the early twentieth century the Liberal Government was heavily involved in calls for social reform. Why not also votes for women?

"Won't you let me help you John?"

and outdated by many Edwardian men. Women, either by their competence at work, activities in local politics or in voluntary capacities such as church or charity activities, demonstrated that there was little to fear that women's political interests would detract from their traditional role as wives and mothers. Change seemed inevitable and in the words of Martin Pugh:

> *…their participation in local government made women's exclusion from national elections increasingly untenable [impossible to defend].*
>
> Martin Pugh, 'Votes for Women', 1990

Why did women want the vote?

Put simply, women wanted the vote as a lever to force greater change. They argued that parliament would never listen to their needs for greater reform in the home and at work until they had a means of making MPs and the government take notice. Lydia Becker expressed this viewpoint in 'The Political Disabilities of Women' in 1872 when she wrote:

> ...the sufferings and the wrongs of women will never be considered worthy of attention by the Legislature [parliament] until they are in possession of the suffrage, and not until they are politically on the same level as men, will their education and their welfare receive equal care from the Government.
>
> Lydia Becker, 1872

The women's suffrage campaign is an overall title covering many different organisations with different methods and motives. In the middle of the nineteenth century suffrage societies, not linked to any political programme and committed to peaceful campaigning, were prominent. By the end of the century each major political party had its own female suffrage group, though it was the more militant and violent suffragettes that grabbed the headlines in the early years of the twentieth century.

Nevertheless, all these groups had one political goal – the right to vote. With the vote women would have a political voice and a tool to combat the legal, economic and social difficulties oppressing women's lives.

However, even among those women who did want reform, not all wanted the vote for the same reasons and there was disagreement over which women should be enfranchised. Should only single women get the vote? Should only married women who were property owners be allowed to vote? Should all adult men and women have the right to vote?

The differing motives

Different groups of women wanted the right to vote for different reasons. For upper class and most middle class women, social success was marked by a good marriage and producing male heirs. To escape from this prison of conformity, women in these classes saw the vote as recognition of their own identity, a way of winning some freedom to fulfil themselves and to use their potential to benefit society and themselves.

Single, middle class women saw the vote as a means of opening up opportunities in a world where they might not 'make a good marriage', since by 1901 there was a 'surplus' of over 1 million women. As a result, these lower-middle class women would have to fend for themselves. These single women saw gaining the vote as a means of creating greater change, perhaps opening up the professions and other 'suitable' employment.

Working class women needed a political voice to be heard in a world which exploited them ruthlessly. Without it, women had no hope of challenging the conditions of work in factories, farming or in sweated industries which were unhealthy and dangerous. Their wages were very low and hardship, poverty, bad health and early death were almost inevitable. Although exceptions to the rule existed – for example, in Dundee women earned fair wages in the jute factories while their husbands sometimes took on the role of 'househusbands' – the fact remained that working class women had to work and for most the alternative was starvation or the workhouse. Nowhere were women's wages equal to men's.

In conclusion, whether rich or poor, many women across the social spectrum realised that only by winning the vote could they significantly improve their lives and status in society.

Activities

Read the following five statements.

a. Women had made no social or political progress before 1900.

b. Women had made some social but no political progress before 1900.

c. Women were second class citizens in all ways before 1900.

d. Women had made considerable social and some political progress before 1900.

e. Women could not be called second class citizens before 1900.

1 Choose which of the above statements you think is/are correct.

2 Collect as many reasons as you can, either from this book or your own research, to support your choice/choices.

3 For each of the statements that you rejected, explain, with reasons, WHY you rejected them.

4 Be prepared to present your ideas either in writing or in a speech.

The importance of the different campaigning groups

The role of the NUWSS

For pressure groups trying to bring about large scale or political change, efficient, preferably nationally organised, campaigns are vital and in 1897 several local women's suffrage societies united to form the National Union of Women's Suffrage Societies (NUWSS) under the leadership of Millicent Fawcett. The NUWSS believed in moderate, 'peaceful' tactics to win the vote, mainly for middle class property-owning women. Later, the NUWSS was nicknamed the Suffragists in contrast to the Suffragettes.

The campaigning strategy of 'peaceful persuasion' used by the NUWSS has led to a common misconception that the organisation was ineffective, ignored by the government and can therefore be ignored as a significant campaigning group. This was not the case. Although membership remained relatively low, at about 6000 until around 1909, a persuasive campaign of meetings, pamphlets, petitions and parliamentary bills regularly introduced by friendly back-bench MPs, had created a situation where many, if not most, MPs had accepted the principle of women's suffrage. Outside parliament, the NUWSS had success in winning the support of some trade unions for the women's cause. The NUWSS reached an agreement of mutual support with the new Labour Party and the Liberal government became alarmed that with greater support and organisation, the Labour Party could become a real threat to the Liberals' chance of election victory if no change in women's political status was made. The NUWSS also provided a 'home' for women angered by the Suffragettes during their 'wild period', so much so that NUWSS membership totalled 53,000 by 1914. These new recruits seemed to want to stay part of the movement, but not be associated with the violence linked with the Pankhursts and their followers.

Rather cynically, Martin Pugh described the move of women towards the NUWSS and away from the Suffragette excesses as 'probably the one positive contribution of the Pankhursts to winning the vote.'

Source 2.5

This advert for a meeting in Kirkwall, Orkney, in 1871 shows the effort and distance women were prepared to go to get their message across. The speaker came from Galloway in the south of Scotland.

Kirkwall, 27th September 1871.

WOMEN'S SUFFRAGE.
PUBLIC MEETING.

MISS TAYLOUR, of Belmont, Stranraer, Honorary Secretary of the Galloway Society for Women's Suffrage, will deliver a LECTURE on the above subject

IN THE

VOLUNTEER HALL, KIRKWALL,
On Monday Evening, 9th October,

AND IN THE

TOWN HALL, STROMNESS,
On Tuesday Evening, 10th October,
At a Quarter-past 8 o'clock.

After the Lecture, a Petition to Parliament will be submitted to the Meeting, in support of Mr Jacob Bright's Bill for conferring the Franchise on Women Householders who pay Rates.

COLLECTION AT THE DOOR TO DEFRAY EXPENSES.

ORKNEY STEAM NAVIGATION COMPANY
(LIMITED).

Why did women gain the right to vote?

The WSPU – the Suffragettes

Emmeline Pankhurst had been a member of the Manchester branch of the NUWSS but in 1903, with the help of her daughters Christabel and Sylvia, she formed the Women's Social and Political Union (WSPU).

The Pankhursts were frustrated both by the lack of progress achieved by the NUWSS and at how, in the early 1900s, newspapers had lost interest in the issue of women's suffrage and seldom reported meetings. In response to such apparent indifference to the campaigns of the NUWSS, the WSPU adopted the motto 'Deeds Not Words' and used campaign methods intended to breathe new life into the issue of women's suffrage.

The new strategy gained publicity in October 1905 when Sir Edward Grey, a minister in the British government, was heckled noisily. The two WSPU members were arrested after a struggle involving kicking and spitting. The women were sent to prison and the nation was shocked that women were prepared to use violence in an attempt to win the vote. Newspapers immediately took notice, the WSPU was nicknamed the Suffragettes and the organisation had achieved its first objective – publicity.

Source 2.6

A protest against the census by Suffragettes in Dundee.

Source 2.7

When the 1911 census was being taken, Suffragettes in many parts of Britain staged protests, arguing that since they were not recognised as citizens and were not allowed to vote, they should not be counted in the national census.

MARGARET MORRISON, Argyle Cottage, Liberton, Midlothian, and DOROTHEA LYNAS or SMITH, otherwise ELIZABETH DOROTHEA CHALMERS SMITH, 13 Broompark Drive, Dennistoun, Glasgow, you are Indicted at the instance of the Right Honourable ALEXANDER URE, His Majesty's Advocate, and the charge against you is that you did, on 23rd July 1913, break into an unoccupied dwelling-house at No. 6 Park Gardens, Glasgow, and did convey, or cause to be conveyed, thereto a quantity of fire-lighters, firewood, a number of pieces of candles, a quantity of paper, cotton wool, cloth, and a number of tins of paraffin oil, and did place these along with three venetian blinds at or against a wooden door in a passage on the first flat of said house, and this you did with intent to set fire to said door and to burn said house.

WEDNESDAY

When the Liberals won the 1906 general election, many Suffragists were convinced that the new government would give women the franchise. Indeed, the new Prime Minister, Henry Campbell-Bannerman, told a group of Suffragists that he was personally in favour of women having the vote – but added that his cabinet was opposed to the idea. When Campbell-Bannerman died in April 1908 he was replaced by Asquith who was very much against the women's campaign. The NUWSS had already been pressurising the Liberals at by-elections by putting up their own male candidate against Liberals who were opposed to women's suffrage and when Asquith became Prime Minister the Suffragettes effectively declared war on the government.

Violent protests followed with a window smashing campaign aimed at government buildings starting in 1908 and, predictably, the prisons filled with Suffragettes. In Scotland, the most common form of militant attack was on pillar boxes, where acid was poured in to destroy letters. Further Suffragette violence followed in 1913 when Suffragettes tried to burn down the houses of two members of the government who opposed votes for women, and cricket pavilions, racecourse stands and golf clubhouses were set on fire. Farington Hall in Dundee and Leuchars railway station were attacked and many public buildings – including Holyrood Palace – were closed for fear of attack, while security was tightened around others. Even historic buildings, such as Whitekirk Church in East Lothian, were attacked if they were in the constituencies of leading politicians.

However, if the government had thought prison would starve the women of the oxygen of publicity, they were wrong. Instead, women used starvation as a political weapon by going on hunger strike.

In July 1909, Suffragette prisoner Marion Dunlop refused to eat. This began a campaign of hunger strikes, designed to embarrass the government if or when a Suffragette died in custody, thereby providing martyrs for the cause. In Scotland, force feeding was started in Perth Prison where Dr Fergus Watson, who had already used the methods elsewhere, was an officer. Trapped between releasing the women or allowing them to die, the government began to force feed the

Source 2.8

Force feeding of women risked serious injury to the women. It was developed in Scotland in Perth Prison.

prisoners. The methods used were frequently described as torture and serious health complications often arose as a result. In Perth, Fergus Watson was already responsible for the death of a Suffragette from double pneumonia, the result of food getting into her lungs. To make matters worse, the women in Perth were held in solitary confinement. When news leaked out that attempts had been made to feed two women by the rectum there was a storm of protest.

In response to the bad publicity generated by the force feeding of hunger strikers, the government introduced the Prisoner's Temporary Discharge for Ill Health Act. Hunger strikers were left alone until they became ill, then they were released. Once the women had recovered, they were re-arrested, sent back to prison and left there until they completed their sentences. At least that was the theory. Many released women did not await quietly the return of the police. Many women hid and police were bogged down in search and find missions. It seemed both sides were playing with the other, hence the nickname, the Cat and Mouse Act.

It is not true that the Suffragette campaign destroyed all support for the cause of women's suffrage. Although support for the cause decreased, it can be argued that, were it not for the Suffragette campaign, the Liberal Government would not have even discussed women's suffrage before the First World War.

How important were the Suffragettes?

Books, newspaper articles, film and photographs have created a folk memory of police arrest, hunger strikers being force fed and even the creation of a martyr for the cause with the death of Emily Wilding Davison at the 1913 Derby. But were these events crucial to winning the vote? It can be easily argued that the campaigning of the Suffragettes brought the issue of votes for women to crisis point and made the issue into a political 'hot potato' that could not be ignored. But did the campaigns of the Suffragettes do more harm than good? As Lord Robert Cecil said in 1912:

> " *The cause of Woman Suffrage is not as strong in this House today as it was a year ago, and everybody knows the cause. Everyone knows that the reason is purely and simply that certain women have broken the law in a way we all deplore...The way in which certain types of women, easily recognised, have acted in the last year or two, especially in the last few weeks...has brought so much disgrace and discredit upon their sex.*
>
> Lord Robert Cecil, 1912

Even within the WSPU, there was concern over the leadership style of Mrs Pankhurst. As a result of her domineering style and suggestions of greater militancy, 70 women left to form the Women's Freedom League (WFL) in 1907. The WFL was not a meek organisation. It was prepared to break the law, for example, by refusing to pay taxes, but it did not support the WSPU's violent campaign of attacks on property. The result of the disagreement among women over the tactics urged by Mrs Pankhurst was that more and more women left the Suffragettes; all that existed by 1914 was a rump of campaigners committed to the leadership of Mrs Pankhurst.

The actions of the Suffragettes had also mobilised opposing opinions, so much so that the anti-suffrage organisation founded in 1908 had evolved into the much more influential National League for Opposing Woman Suffrage by 1911. Given the diminished scale of the WSPU by 1914, Martin Pugh seems correct when he says that the enduring perception that votes for women were achieved by the Suffragettes is more the result of the Pankhursts' talent for self publicity, even when the organisation they led was losing support at an alarming rate, rather than an effective campaign.

By the summer of 1914, all the leaders of the WSPU were either in prison, unwell or living in hiding. Over 1000 Suffragettes were in prison for destroying public property and public opinion had turned against the group, so much so that by 1913 it was dangerous for any Suffragette to speak out at public meetings. Anti-suffragist picture postcards and popular songs mocked the suffrage movement. By the eve of the First World War there were very few Suffragettes still actively campaigning.

A case can then be made that the Pankhursts' campaign of violence failed to shift the government. In fact, their campaign provided a good excuse for anti-suffrage campaigners to avoid the issue of fairness by focussing on the militant campaign, which seemed to provide an excellent example of why women could not be trusted with the vote. The tactical errors of Mrs Pankhurst also damaged the women's campaign. Her failure to ally with the Labour Party in a campaign to increase democracy in Britain ignored the thousands of working class men who still had no voice and Mrs Pankhurst was even willing to settle for granting the vote to some wealthy women rather than campaign for the vote for all adults. Mrs Pankhurst's policy lost the Suffragettes political allies but gained the anger of working class women.

Finally, when enfranchisement was actually being discussed, the Pankhursts had long since abandoned their campaign and had no influence over the discussion – apart from the possibility of a renewal of Suffragette activity after the war.

In summary, the case of Mrs Pankhurst and the Suffragettes shows that it is useful to remember that those who pioneer a cause are not necessarily responsible for its success.

Why did women gain the right to vote?

The importance of the Great War

Britain declared war on Germany in August 1914 and two days later the NUWSS suspended its political campaigning for the vote. To encourage the Suffragettes to end their campaign, the government released all WSPU prisoners and in response the WSPU agreed to stop their campaign. With a grant of over £2000 from the government (which led to accusations of betrayal from the pacifist Women's Freedom League and more militant Suffragettes), a WSPU pro-war propaganda campaign encouraged men to join the armed forces and women to demand 'the right to serve' with slogans such as 'For Men Must Fight and Women Must Work'. The WSPU even changed the name of their newspaper from *The Suffragette* to *Britannia*. Mrs Pankhurst now wrapped herself in patriotism rather than feminism.

Women's war work was important to Britain's eventual victory. As casualty rates increased on the battlefield and conscription was introduced to swell the ranks, women were needed to fill the gaps on the home front. Industries that had previously excluded women now welcomed them. Women worked as conductors on trams and buses, as typists and secretaries and nearly 200,000 women found work in government departments. Thousands worked on farms, at the docks and even in the police. The biggest increase in female employment was in the

Source 2.9

When war broke out the WSPU ceased their campaign and urged women to 'do their bit' for the war effort, such as this female motorcycle courier.

38

previously male-dominated engineering industry. Over 700,000 women were employed making munitions and facing considerable danger, not just from explosions but also from the chemicals they used. But has the importance of the Great War to the cause of women's suffrage been exaggerated? Did votes for women remain a 'live' issue during the war, or did other factors move the government towards votes for women in 1918?

The political debate about giving women the right to vote is dealt with in the democracy section on pages 20–22. Here is a summary of the main points:

- Did women get the vote because of their war work?

Women who worked long hours and risked their lives in munitions factories were mostly single, in their late teens or early twenties. The women who were given the vote were 'respectable' ladies, aged 30 or over, who were property owners or married to property owners.

- Was political stability the reason?

Protests and demonstrations in 'Red Clydeside' had led to tanks and soldiers in the streets of Glasgow. Ordinary working class women across Glasgow had organised the effective rent strikes of 1915. Could the government risk a resumption of social disorder among women who resented being pressured into returning to 'women's work' after the war? During the war many women had become aware of their own influence and ability to make changes to improve their living and working conditions. Could the government be sure that these women would not join a revitalised Suffragette campaign after the war and return to Suffragette 'terrorism'?

- Was some change made in order to prevent even greater demands?

Many MPs did believe that some reform was inevitable and that passing the female suffrage section of the 1918 Representation of the People Act would keep the Suffragists happy but also delay more radical reform – such as full and equal voting rights for men and women. A general view at the time was that such equality could be postponed for up to 30 years if the 1918 bill was passed with a section allowing limited female suffrage.

The vote at last

At the beginning of 1917, a plan to enfranchise women was being seriously discussed by MPs and a bill was introduced in March 1918 to give women the vote on the same terms as men. That idea was rejected, but on 28 March 1917 the House of Commons voted 341 to 62 that women over the age of 30 who were householders, the wives of householders, occupiers of property with an annual rent of £5, or graduates of British universities should have the vote.

Why did women gain the right to vote?

The 1918 Representation of the People Act also gave all men over the age of 21 the right to vote (and aged 19 if they had been on active service in the armed forces). The electorate increased to about 21 million of which 8.4 million were women – about 40 per cent of the total voters.

Equal voting rights

At the time, the 1918 Representation of the People Act seemed a major victory for the Suffragist movement. However, there were women who still saw the new law as a betrayal as it still classed them as second class citizens to men. Politically, women were still not the equal to men in Britain. Men could vote on an age qualification alone and nine years earlier than women, who still had to 'qualify'. Even then, about 22 per cent of women 30 years of age and above were denied the right to vote as they were not property owners. These women were usually working class, although the new middle class 'flapper', tasting independence away from parents in rented flats, also had no vote.

Source 2.10

Some women finally gained the vote in 1918. But did women's lives improve hugely because of it?

AT LAST

However, the politicians were happy. The NUWSS and WSPU disbanded. A new organisation called the National Union of Societies for Equal Citizenship was established, campaigning for the same voting rights as men, equal pay, fairer divorce laws and an end to discrimination against women in the professions, but it posed no threat of civil disorder to the government.

Ten years later, there was little opposition to the extension of the franchise to all women on the same terms as men. The heat had gone out of the issue and there seemed no reason to object to the further reform.

By 1928 most of the original campaigners for women's suffrage were dead. All except Millicent Fawcett. She was in parliament to see the 1928 Representation of the People Act passed and wrote in her diary:

 It is almost exactly 61 years ago since I heard John Stuart Mill introduce his suffrage amendment to the Reform Bill on May 20th, 1867. So I have had extraordinary good luck in having seen the struggle from the beginning.

Millicent Fawcett, 1928

Activities

Teach a lesson

In groups of three or four, your target is to teach a lesson to the rest of your class which is linked to the issue of votes for women. Your main resource for information is this textbook but you must also research, find, beg or borrow other resources to make your lesson come alive. Think of the times you have been bored just listening to someone talk. Your lesson must be different!

- Negotiate with your teacher/tutor how long you have to prepare this lesson.

- Your lesson should be presented in an organised, interesting, mature and informative way.

- Planning is vital – and all in your group must participate. It would be helpful to assign tasks such as a gopher to go get materials, a timekeeper to watch how your time is being used, a facilitator to keep things running smoothly in your group (tact and diplomacy needed here!) and a recorder to note ideas and what was suggested before you all forget.

- Your lesson should last between 5 and 10 minutes.

- It must have visual material – PowerPoint or OHP are possibilities.

As in any lesson there are really important things for you to decide and aim for:

- What do you want your students to be able to do and know at the end of your lesson?

- How will you assess the success of your lesson – in other words, what will you expect to see or hear your students doing to prove your lesson has been successful?

Sample Essay Questions

1 To what extent was the Suffragist campaign effective in gaining votes for women?

2 Why were some women given the right to vote in 1918?

3 'The Suffragettes were more successful at gaining headlines than achieving real progress for women's political rights.' To what extent can this view be supported?

Why did women gain the right to vote?

Why did the Liberal reforms happen?

This issue focuses on the reasons why the Liberal Government of 1906–1914 passed so many reforms to help the old, the young, the sick, and the unemployed.

Was the Government reflecting changing public attitudes, or were the reforms much more politically motivated? Was the Government persuaded that the 'deserving poor' deserved government help? Or was the Government much more concerned about the safety and security of the country?

Source 3.1

By Edwardian times, old attitudes about the 'deserving poor' were beginning to change. The work of charitable organisations alerted people to the problems of destitute children, whose poverty was through no fault of their own.

What were nineteenth-century attitudes to poverty?

In the later nineteenth century, public and government attitudes towards poverty and how to help the poor changed considerably. Government policy towards most social issues was called 'laissez faire'. The phrase means to leave alone, and the feeling that the poor should look after themselves was at the core of Samuel Smiles' book *Self Help*.

Source 3.2

In the mid-nineteenth century, poverty was seen as a personal failure.
Self help was the answer, according to Samuel Smiles.

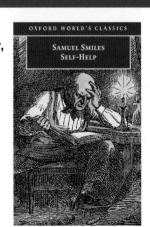

OXFORD WORLD'S CLASSICS

SAMUEL SMILES
SELF-HELP

Smiles wrote that 'self help is the root of all genuine growth'. He meant that an individual had the obligation to look after himself and his family through effort and determination. Smiles, and others in mid-Victorian Britain, believed poverty was a sign of personal weakness, either as a result of idleness or genetic inheritance. Norman Pearson, a late nineteenth century voice on the topic of poverty, believed that the poor were 'seldom capable of reform' and that they tended to be 'made of inferior material... and cannot be improved'. He also argued that the poor were poor 'in their blood and their bones' and that they should be prevented from breeding!

It was as if the poor were being treated as criminals; their crime being poverty. The Scottish Poor House and the Workhouse in England existed to help the absolutely destitute, but these places were feared and hated as institutions that signalled a person's failure. To enter such places was shameful and to be avoided at all cost. As a result, many of the poor depended on charity organisations.

Philanthropy – meaning individuals doing good works to help the less fortunate – was a strong theme running through Victorian and Edwardian society. The wealthier sections of society felt it was their moral duty to help the poor, encouraged by a strong Christian belief that it was 'better to give than to receive'. As a report of the Hackney Benevolent Pension Society put it:

Source 3.3

The Barony Parish Poorhouse at Barnhill was described in 1882 as 'a very capacious asylum for the children of poverty and well adapted by its cleanliness, ventilation and position to mitigate [ease] the ills of their condition'. It was Scotland's largest poorhouse.

> " *To soothe the sorrows of the poor and to support the infirmities of the aged...these are duties which are encouraged by the clearest dictates of our religion.*

Hackney Benevolent Pension Society Report

Recent studies have questioned the effectiveness of these charitable organisations. Each organisation seemed to work in isolation, knowing nothing of the work of other groups outwith their own immediate area. The lack of a 'big picture' to see who was being helped, where and by whom, on a national basis led to duplication of effort. Contemporary historian J.R. Green observed that there were hundreds of agencies at work over the same ground with no co-operation between them. Partly in response to the fears

Why did the Liberal reforms happen?

that individuals could apply more than once for help to different organisations, the Charity Organisation Society (COS) was created in 1869. Their attitude was typical of later Victorian attitudes towards poverty.

 ...the poor should meet all the ordinary contingencies [expenses] of life, relying not upon public and private charity, but upon their own industry [hard work] and thrift [savings]. It is a hurtful misuse of money to spend on assisting the labouring classes to meet emergencies which they should have anticipated and provided for.

> Charity Organisation Society

This view was echoed by former Prime Minister William Gladstone who said in 1884:

 There is a disposition to think...that the government ought to do everything...The spirit of self reliance should be preserved in the minds of the masses of the people, in the minds of every member of that class.

> William Gladstone, 1884

Changing attitudes to poverty

In contrast to the beliefs of the COS, it was becoming increasingly clear that the poor could not deal with circumstances beyond their control. The assumption that poverty was in some way the fault of the individual was being questioned more and more.

A report from the Macclesfield Relief Association concluded:

 How almost impossible is it, then, for a working man to be thrifty? He lives from hand-to-mouth...Directly sickness comes, or a few months of abnormally bad trade, there is nothing to fall back on; and what can our Relief Society do when there are several hundreds in similar plight?

> Macclesfield Relief Association

In 1889 the writer George Sims argued the case for government intervention.

There is a penalty for packing cattle too closely together: why should there be none for improperly housing men and women and children? The law says that no child shall grow up without reading, writing and arithmetic; but the law does nothing that children may have air, and light, and shelter.

> George Sims, 1889

While charitable organisations might help individuals temporarily, there was a recognition that such charities did little to reach long term solutions. One writer described charity as doing nothing more 'than manuring the ground in which these social weeds grow'.

With rather more tact, the Reverend L.R. Phelps of Oxford said in 1901:

> 66 *Private philanthropy cannot provide a remedy for widespread want which results from broad and general social causes; it ought not be expected to do so; the provision of such remedies is the responsibility of the state and should be accepted as such.*
>
> L.R. Phelps, 1901

This statement alone illustrates the change in attitude towards social problems generally – an attitude which saw the solution lying with the government, or state, rather than the individual.

Why did the Liberal Government take action against poverty?

In any answer to this question there are six important sections that must be considered:

1 The reports of Booth and Rowntree
2 Worries about national security
3 Concerns over national efficiency
4 Political advantage
5 New Liberalism
6 The effect of Municipal Socialism

The reports of Booth and Rowntree

At the end of the nineteenth century, investigations revealed the true, and mainly unsuspected, levels of poverty in Britain. These investigations proved that poverty had causes, often beyond the control of the poor themselves. Poverty restricted the ability of men, and especially of women, children and the elderly, to control their lives. What could any individual do about low pay, unemployment, sickness and old age?

There were many investigations into living conditions but two particular investigations had a big impact on political thinking.

The first was organised and run by Charles Booth, a London businessman who doubted the claims of socialists that a quarter of

Source 3.4

Why was Charles Booth's report on London life so influential to the thinking about poverty?

the population lived in extreme poverty. Booth decided to investigate poverty in the East End of the city. Working with a team of researchers, mainly at weekends and evenings, Booth's work was based on hard, statistical facts – not opinion. In 1889 he published his shocking results as *Labour and Life of the People*. The book showed that 35 per cent of London's population lived in extreme poverty, much worse than the socialists had claimed.

Booth then decided to research all of London and over the next twelve years, between 1891 and 1903, Booth published his findings. In seventeen volumes entitled *Life and Labour of the People of London*, Booth presented the same levels of poverty. He then argued that poverty was such a big problem that only the government could really help. If nothing was done to improve the lives of the poor, Booth argued, Britain was in danger of a socialist revolution.

The second investigation into poverty was carried out by Seebohm Rowntree in the city of York. Inspired by the work of Booth in London, Rowntree decided to find out if London's level of poverty applied to that city only or if similar levels of poverty existed across Britain.

After two years of research, Rowntree published *Poverty, A Study of Town Life* in 1901 which showed that almost 30 per cent of the York population lived in extreme poverty.

People realised that if York, a relatively small, 'typical' English city, hid such problems then so would other British cities and that the problem of poverty was therefore a national problem.

In his research, Rowntree defined poverty very closely. He drew up a 'poverty line' which was the least amount a family could survive on. He also defined poverty as either 'primary' or 'secondary'. In the former, a family lacked sufficient earnings to buy even the minimum necessities. In the latter definition, poverty was the result of earning enough to stay above the poverty line, but then 'wasting' some money on items such as alcohol, gambling or smoking. However, Rowntree recognised that such 'wasteful' spending might well be 'escapes', the need for which was caused by poverty itself.

Source 3.5

Rowntree's report on poverty in York shocked people. Why?

Rowntree also argued that poverty might not be constant, with families and individuals dropping below the poverty line at different stages in their life, especially old age.

The reports of Charles Booth and Seebohm Rowntree provided politicians with evidence to suggest that no matter how hard certain people tried, they could not lift themselves out of poverty. Poverty was shown by the reports to have causes, the cures for which were beyond the individual efforts of the poor. The concept of the 'deserving poor', those who were poor through no fault of their own, took root and was an important theme running through the Liberal reforms.

Worries about national security

In 1899, Britain became involved in a war in South Africa, which was part of the British Empire at that time.

Since Britain had a relatively small army, volunteer recruits were needed to swell the ranks. However, the Government became alarmed when almost 25 per cent of the volunteers were

Source 3.6

The poor health of volunteer recruits during the Boer war led to concerns about national security.

rejected because they were physically unfit to serve in the armed forces. This figure was even higher among volunteers from the industrial cities. Politicians and the public alike began to ask if Britain could survive a war, or protect its

empire against a far stronger enemy than the South African Boers, if the nation's 'fighting stock' of young men was so unhealthy.

As a direct result of these concerns, an Interdepartmental Committee on Physical Deterioration was created to examine the problem of ill health in England and Wales, while in Scotland a Royal Commission did the same task. Their reports in 1904 suggested that the physical condition of many adult males was poor and made recommendations about improving diet and overcrowding. More specifically, they recommended free school meals and medical examinations for school children. Since these points were among the first reforms introduced by the Liberals after their election victory in 1906, it is clear that concern over national security had a direct influence on the reforms.

Source 3.7

If young men were too unfit to serve in the army, what would happen to Britain's security?

Concerns over national efficiency

By the end of the nineteenth century, Britain was no longer the strongest industrial nation and was facing serious competition from new industrial nations such as Germany. It was believed that if the health and educational standards of Britain's workers got worse, Britain's position as a strong industrial power would be threatened.

There was also concern that in times of economic depression unemployment soared in certain areas while jobs existed in others. Politicians such as Winston Churchill voiced concern that part of the problem was that the unemployed did not know where the new jobs were. This, he argued, was an example of inefficiency weakening Britain's industrial output. A few years later the Liberals opened the first labour exchanges to minimise the time a worker was unemployed, thereby increasing the efficiency of the labour market.

Another development which may have influenced attitudes was that in Germany a system of welfare benefits and old age pensions had already been set up in the 1880s. Why could Britain not do likewise?

Political advantage and New Liberalism

Many historians believe that the Liberal reforms were not passed because of genuine concern about the poor but simply for political advantage. From 1884, most working class men had the vote and the Liberals had tended to attract many of those votes. But by 1906 the newly-formed Labour Party was competing for the same votes. So how justified is the claim that the Liberal reforms happened for the very selfish reason of simply retaining working class votes?

Liberals had always argued that liberalism stood for individual freedom with the least possible involvement of the government in the lives of ordinary people. 'Old Liberal' attitudes believed poverty was due to personal defects of character, but as the realisation grew that poverty itself imposed restrictions on the choices available to an individual, a new definition of Liberalism grew up. New Liberals argued that state intervention was necessary to liberate people from social problems over which they had no control.

Source 3.8

The Lib-Lab alliance between Liberals and Labour would not last forever. How badly would Liberal votes be damaged if Labour competed directly?

In truth, the nature of Liberalism was changing long before the formation of the Labour Party in 1900. There were disagreements over the extent of reform but Liberal politicians were moving towards a reforming programme. There were, of course, a large number of Liberals who were wary about reform but they were willing to swallow their concerns if it meant they could gain more working class votes. The party had, after all, been out of power since 1886.

Nevertheless, New Liberal ideas were not important issues in the general election campaign of 1905. In fact, the Liberals made no mention of social reforms in their party manifesto. When the Liberals took over the government in 1906 some reforms were introduced – mostly associated with the public concern over national security – but only when 'Old Liberal' Prime Minister Campbell Bannerman died in 1908 did the door open for new 'interventionist' ideas. When Prime Minister Asquith appointed New Liberals such as David Lloyd George and Winston Churchill to top jobs, suddenly a flood of social reforms were put into place.

The effect of Municipal Socialism

During the second half of the nineteenth century the public had become used to increasing levels of local and national government intervention in their lives.

The improvements carried out by local (municipal) authorities were paid for by a form of local taxation which was used to improve the lives of people in their local area. Of course the wealthy paid most, but it was the poor who gained most benefit. In this sense a basic socialist idea of redistributing wealth between rich and poor, managed by the local authority, could be seen in operation. It was for this reason that local authority action to use local taxation income for social improvement was called Municipal Socialism.

Nationally, a host of laws improved working and living conditions, such as Factory Acts and Public Health Acts. Governments of various parties moved towards greater intervention. In fact, writers at the time wrote about the tendency of local authorities to provide everything the population required in its passage from the cradle to the grave, a phrase usually associated with the Labour Government's reforms of 40 years later.

It was in the growing towns and cities that some Liberal-controlled local authorities became deeply involved in programmes of social welfare. In 1873, Liberal Joseph Chamberlain became mayor of Birmingham and for the next three years he used his influence in municipal politics to introduce a series of social reforms.

Birmingham's water supply was considered a danger to public health. Piped water was only supplied three days per week and half of the city's population was dependent on well water, much of which was polluted by sewage. In answer to the problem, Chamberlain purchased Birmingham's waterworks and also the gas works. He then went on to clear away many of

Birmingham's slums. Chamberlain became known nationally, mainly due to his brand of 'municipal socialism'. In the words of one report, he left Birmingham 'parked, paved, gas and watered and improved'.

City authorities spent money on improving a wide range of services. Hospitals were established and attempts were made to improve housing, although as late as 1886 Glasgow still had a third of its families living in one-roomed houses. By the 1850s, Glasgow Town Council had control of the city water supply and by the 1860s was involved in providing gas street lighting.

Public parks were opened to provide access to fresh air and relaxation and libraries were opened to provide access to education and 'self improvement.' By 1903 it was observed that a Glaswegian could:

> *...live in a municipal house; he may walk along the municipal street, or ride on the municipal tramcar and watch the municipal dust-cart collecting refuse which is to be used to fertilise the municipal farm. Then he may turn into the municipal market, buy a steak from an animal killed in the municipal slaughterhouse, and cook it by the municipal gas stove. For his recreation he can choose amongst municipal libraries, municipal art galleries and municipal music in municipal parks. Should he fall ill, he can ring his doctor on the municipal telephone, or he may be taken to the municipal hospital in the municipal ambulance by a municipal policeman. Should he be so unfortunate as to get on fire, he will be put out by a municipal fireman, using municipal water; after which he will, perhaps, forego the enjoyment of a municipal bath, though he may find it necessary to get a new suit in the municipal old clothes market.*
>
> Unknown commentator, 1903

Long before national government got involved in social reforms to improve the lives of citizens, local authorities were well on the way to doing so in many towns and cities. Such a trend towards social reform and government control can be considered a factor in setting the scene for the Liberal reforms.

Activities

1   Create two lists.

You are a supporter of 'laissez faire' in 1900. Create a list of reasons why the national government should not get involved in helping the poor.

You are a supporter of municipal socialism and think the idea of publicly funded state help should spread nationally. Create a list of reasons why the government should help the poor – or at least the 'deserving poor'.

2   Be prepared to explain what you think the phrase 'deserving poor' means in the context of early twentieth-century social reforms.

3   Tutorial topic: If there was such a thing as 'the deserving poor' there must have been those who were thought of as 'the undeserving poor'. What sort of people do you think would be classed as undeserving poor? Why would many people, then and now, argue that the undeserving poor should not be helped by the government? Be prepared to explain your ideas and suport your argument with reasoned evidence.

Essay Writing

How far was concern over national security the real reason for the Liberal reforms passed between 1906 and 1914?

This essay is called 'an isolated factor' essay. The essay title provides one possible reason why the Liberal reforms happened and you are asked if you agree with that view or if other reasons should be considered. You have to decide if national security was the real reason why the Liberal reforms happened or if other reasons were more important.

You know there are six reasons listed in this chapter to explain why the Liberal reforms were passed. The essay only asks about one of them. Or does it?

The title offers one reason and a reasonable answer will start by saying fears over national security 'partly' explain the reforms. Then you must argue there were other influences on the government. Your essay should explain and show off what you know (develop) about each of the influences on the government before reaching a conclusion.

continued ➔

Why did the Liberal reforms happen?

Essay Writing *continued*

Here is an example of a very weak introduction:

In order to answer this question it is necessary to explain why the Liberal reforms happened and decide if national security was a main reason. The Liberal reforms began in 1906 and were passed to help the old, the young, the sick and the unemployed.

Why is this a very weak introduction?

● It is far too short – only two sentences long.

● This introduction does nothing to help the writer. Time is wasted by writing out the words of the question. All this does is pretend to be an introduction.

● There is no thought here about how the essay will develop.

● There is no signposting of any ideas about why the reforms happened.

● The second sentence is completely irrelevant by writing about the reforms, suggesting the writer has not understood the question.

Here is a much better introduction:

By the early twentieth century the Liberal Government was concerned that Britain was losing its status as a major industrial and military power. Concern over national efficiency (1) and security (2) played a part in persuading the Government that reforms were needed. However, other reasons also played a part. The new Labour Party promised social reform and the Liberals were worried about losing votes. A way had to found of keeping the working class votes (3). Reform could therefore be seen as a rather selfish, politically advantageous response to political change. The Liberal reforms were also partly the result of concern for the poor. The reports of Booth and Rowntree had argued that 1/3 of Britain's population lived in poverty (4). Changing attitudes within the party, summed up as New Liberalism (5), were influential in promoting change and the example of municipal socialism (6) encouraged Liberal politicians towards national reforms.

continued ➡

Essay Writing *continued*

Why is this a better introduction?

- It is an appropriate length. The style is mature and clearly signposts the points to be raised in the essay. If it helps, there is no reason why you cannot *faintly* number your separate points with a pencil (as in the example above) as a guide to yourself for what the main development paragraphs should be about.

- It provides a structure which the candidate can follow through the rest of the essay.

- There is no irrelevance and it is clear to a marker the candidate has understood the question.

What makes a good conclusion?

A suitable conclusion is a paragraph at the end of your essay that makes clear you are summing up your essay and providing a final overall answer to the question. It should last about 5 or 6 lines of a regular essay and preferably start with words such as 'Finally...' or 'In conclusion...'

Throughout your essay you should have been arguing a case and perhaps weighing up different reasons to explain why the Liberal reforms happened. You should have explained why concern over national security was an important reason but you should also have considered other reasons why the reforms happened. In your conclusion you have to make up your mind and answer the main question.

Here are three examples of possible conclusions.

This is a weak conclusion:

The Liberal reforms happened because the politicians were concerned about the poor. Booth and Rowntree proved that people were poor through no fault of their own and the reforms aimed to help the old, the young, the sick and the unemployed.

Why is this a weak conclusion?

It is weak because it does not make clear it is a conclusion. It makes an unsupported statement that simply states a reason but ignores the focus of the original question. There is no balance here summing up the other reasons nor any attempt to decide which were the most important reasons. It is also irrelevant to mention the reforms that were later passed – they have no place in an essay on why the reforms happened.

continued

Here is a better conclusion:

In conclusion, the Liberal reforms were the result of many issues. Concern over national security was one of them. There was also concern over reports of widespread poverty in Britain, as well as new political ideas and winning political advantage over the new Labour Party which had been formed in 1900 and was competing for votes from the working classes who had gained votes in 1884. By 1906 the Liberals were afraid they might lose votes.

Why is this a better conclusion, but not a good one?

It starts by making clear this is the conclusion. It sums up points that have been developed earlier in the essay, but then it continues to give information that is detailed, new and irrelevant. The creation of the Labour Party was perhaps an influence on the Liberals but details about it certainly should not appear in the conclusion summing up those influences. The place to put that detail is in the appropriate development paragraph earlier in the essay.

Here is a very good conclusion:

In conclusion, the Liberal reforms were the result of many influences. Political willingness to pass reforms was influenced by new ideas about state intervention and New Liberalism. Fears of losing votes to the new Labour Party may have made the reforms a more pressing necessity. Meanwhile, concern about Britain's national security and position in the world made politicians realise that a healthier working class was necessary. However, without the reports of Booth and Rowntree making people aware of dire poverty in Britain perhaps the Liberals would not have responded with a programme of reforms. These reports made people realise that poverty was often beyond the individual's ability to help themselves and the concept of the deserving poor requiring assistance was at the core of the Liberal reforms.

Why is this a very good conclusion?

This conclusion meets all the requirements of a conclusion. It is clearly marked as the conclusion. It sums up the main issues developed in the essay. At the same time, it prioritises the reasons by suggesting some were much more influential than others. Finally, the quality of written English, the vocabulary, the awareness of essay structure and an argued case puts this well into the A pass category.

4 How successful were the Liberal reforms?

Between 1906 and 1914, the Liberal Government introduced a series of reforms that tried to help the young, the sick, the old and the unemployed. To deal successfully with this issue you must be able to do two things:

1 Be able to describe the Liberal reforms. Which group in society did each reform try to help? How did each reform try to help?
2 Be able to judge how successful the reforms were.

Did the reforms do what they set out to do? What were the good and not so good parts of each reform? Were some reforms more successful than others? Why did the Liberals seem to ignore some serious social problems?

The reforms dealing with children

School meals

By 1906, the problem of children being too hungry or generally too weak to learn was well known. A pamphlet written in 1885 by Amie Hicks declared:

I would work for and support one good free meal a day...It is impossible to educate half-starved or insufficiently fed children without physical and mental injury...It is impossible for our working classes to ensure their children proper nourishment.

Amie Hicks, 1885

Twenty years later nothing had changed when the Committee on Physical Deterioration reported:

It is the height of cruelty to subject half starved children to the process of education.

Committee on Physical Deterioration, 1905

In 1906, the Liberals won a landslide victory and became the Government, but at the same time several Labour MPs were elected, one of whom was Fred Jowett, MP for Bradford. For some time Jowett and Margaret McMillan had been providing illegal school meals in Bradford – illegal in the sense they had no right to do so since the meals were paid for by local taxation. Jowett's maiden speech was on the subject of school meals, arguing that since the

Government had made education compulsory, it must take responsibility for the proper nourishment of school children. The new Liberal Government was convinced and in 1906 it passed the Provision of School Meals Act. Local authorities were permitted to raise money by increasing rates (a local tax based on property values) but the law did not force local authorities to provide school meals. By 1911, less than a third of all education authorities were using rates to support school meal provision and almost 30 years later over half of all local authorities still were not providing the service. Clearly, the Liberals had acknowledged the problem but had not forced through a solution.

Medical inspection

Building on concerns about the health of the nation exposed by the unfitness of army recruits to fight the Boers in South Africa, the 1906 Report of the Inter-Departmental Committee on Medical Inspection and Feeding of Children Attending Public Elementary Schools stated that:

> *[in cases where the] school medical officer inspected each child referred to him by teachers as suffering from defects likely to affect their education, e.g. defects of sight, uncleanliness, infectious disease, physical unfitness to attend, there have been specially beneficial results regarding eyesight and infectious disease.*

Report of the Inter-Departmental Committee on Medical Inspection and Feeding of Children Attending Public Elementary Schools, 1906

However, the report continued:

> *The local authority inspected but did not provide treatment. Owing to poverty, a large percentage of cases went untreated.*

The Liberal Government was well aware of the problems facing Britain in the future if the health of most of its children did not improve, so in 1907 medical inspections for children were made compulsory. At least three inspections were to happen during a child's school career, but as critics pointed out there was no provision for the treatment of illnesses or infections found, nor was there

Source 4.1

A medical inspection of school children – checking for lice.

any attempt to improve the health of older children or adults. This was a very limited measure, the reason for which is revealed in the quotation from the Inter-Departmental Committee. Their task was to report whether help 'to improve the health of children could be better organised, without any charge upon public funds'. Cost, rather than good health, was the prime concern.

Medical inspection did little to solve any problems so it was not until free medical treatment for school children began in 1912 that problems could be dealt with.

The Children's Charter

Children were accepted as the group least able to protect themselves from poverty and associated social 'evils'. Born into poverty, many children were believed to be victims of their circumstances and therefore judged to be 'deserving poor'. Poor children were often forced into hazardous work and abused or neglected at home.

While cruelty to animals was an offence punishable by law, children had no such defence under Victorian law.

Source 4.2

The Children's Charter was a collection of laws to help children. In what ways did they help?

Protecting children and young people: The Charter

Early attempts to protect children from 'social evils', such as cigarettes and alcohol, by setting minimum ages at which these things could be bought, had limited success. The result was that in 1908 a Children's Act brought together the many rulings and decisions made in the past, all designed to protect children from neglect and abuse. While the Act ensured children were not living on the streets without food or education, the law also banned children under 16 from smoking, drinking alcohol, or begging.

New juvenile courts were set up for children accused of committing crimes. Remand homes were opened for children who were awaiting trial, rather than putting them in adult prisons. Borstals were set up to deal with children convicted of breaking the law in order to keep them away from adult criminals. When released from a borstal, probation officers were employed to help and advise the former offenders in an attempt to avoid re-offending.

All these reforms were collectively called the 'Children's Charter' because it was believed this set of reforms would be like an old fashioned document or charter which would guarantee better lives for children.

How successful were the Liberal reforms?

The Charter contained many new pieces of legislation and some parts of it were difficult to enforce while others took time to put into place. The time taken to enforce all the legislation meant the Children's Charter only helped improve conditions for some children during the period from 1906 to 1914.

Helping the old

Seebohm Rowntree was only one of many social reformers who argued that something should be done to help the poor who were doomed to become even poorer when they became too old to work. Charles Booth had earlier recommended old age pensions and as Lloyd George, Chancellor of the Exchequer, said:

 It is rather a shame...to allow those who have toiled all their days to end in penury and possibly starvation. It is rather hard that an old workman should have to find his way to the gates of the tomb...through the brambles and thorns of poverty. The provision [of pensions] for the aged and deserving poor – it was time it was done.

Lloyd George, 1909

Lloyd George believed the best way to help was to guarantee an income to people who were too old to work and this was done in 1908 with the Old Age Pensions Act.

People over 70 were given between one shilling (five pence) and five shillings (25 pence) a week depending on any income they might have. Once a person over 70 had income above twelve shillings (60 pence) a week, their entitlement to a pension stopped. Married couples were given 37 pence (seven shillings and six pence).

The Liberals hailed old age pensions as a great success.

The description of an old lady collecting her pension at the post office and saying, 'Thank goodness for that Lord George' (she naively thought only someone as great as a Lord could be so generous), taken from Flora Thompson's novel *Lark Rise to Candleford*, is often used to support the claim that old age pensions were a huge benefit to the poor. Lloyd George himself described the reform as part of a Liberal campaign:

Source 4.3

This cartoon attacks Lloyd George and shows him as a robber. Why would some people agree with that view?

THE PHILANTHROPIC HIGHWAYMAN.
Mr. Lloyd-George. "I'LL MAKE 'EM PITY THE AGED POOR!"

> **"** *...to wage implacable warfare against poverty and squalidness. I cannot help hoping and believing that before this generation has passed away, we shall have advanced a great step towards that good time, when poverty...will be as remote to the people of this country as the wolves which once infested its forests.*
>
> Lloyd George, 1909

But just how realistic were these claims of success?

Rowntree's own study had identified that the bare minimum income to stop a person from falling below his primary poverty line was 35 pence (seven shillings) a week and a married couple required 58 pence (eleven shillings and eight pence). Clearly the old age pension came nowhere near meeting the basic needs of the elderly poor.

Labour politicians argued that the level of benefits was too low and that few of the genuinely poor would live till their 70th birthday. Life expectancy in the worst industrial slums was in the mid-40s, and working people suffered the ageing effects of harsh working and living conditions. By their early 50s most were too old to continue hard physical work.

Many had hoped the pension would be paid to all the elderly, but when the details were announced there were complaints that many of the old were excluded from claiming a pension because they failed to meet several qualification rules. These rules were that no person who had claimed poor relief in the previous year or had been in prison in the previous two years could claim a pension. Nor could people who had failed to work regularly.

It can easily be argued that the amounts of money given as a pension were not enough to prevent poverty but by 1914 there were 970,000 claimants. The Old Age Pensions Act may not have solved the problem of poverty for the elderly but it did make life slightly better.

Helping the sick

In 1911 there was no free National Health Service. The poor generally could not afford medical help, especially as they lost wages during absence from work. Illness was recognised as a major cause of poverty.

Source 4.4

The National Insurance Act provided real help for workers facing difficulties through ill health or unemployment.

To ease the problem of poverty through illness or unemployment, the Chancellor of the Exchequer, David Lloyd George, introduced the National Insurance Act which created a system of insurance against illness and unemployment. In 1908, Lloyd George had visited Germany and had seen for himself the German insurance system established twenty years earlier. He returned, convinced of the need to assist workers who had fallen on hard times through no fault of their own. In his budget speeech in 1909 he argued that since Germany, Britain's rival in the years leading to the First World War, could provide a national insurance scheme for its workers, why could Britain not do likewise and put itself on 'a level with Germany, and not emulate [copy] them only in armaments'.

The 1911 National Insurance Act was in two parts. Part 1 created a scheme of unemployment insurance and a labour exchange scheme. Part 2 was a health insurance scheme. The money paid to claimants was provided by contributions from the person insured, the government and the employer.

The National Insurance Scheme of 1911 applied to workers aged between 16 and 60 earning less than £160 a year – about 15 million people. The scheme was called a contributory system since each worker paid four pence a week towards the help they received. The employer paid three pence a week and the government paid two pence a week. That meant each insured worker got nine pence in benefits from an outlay of four pence. Lloyd George himself popularised the scheme with the slogan 'ninepence for fourpence'.

An insured worker got ten shillings a week (50 pence) when off sick, but the benefits only lasted for 26 weeks. A sickness benefit of ten shillings (50 pence) per week was paid for thirteen weeks. Women received less – only 35 pence. After thirteen weeks the benefit was reduced to only five shillings (25 pence) a week for a further thirteen weeks. Other help for insured workers was a 30 shillings (one pound and 50 pence) maternity grant and free medical treatment including medicines.

Those workers who contributed were also guaranteed seven shillings a week for fifteen weeks in any one year when they were unemployed. The benefits were paid at the recently-opened Labour Exchanges which provided unemployed workers with information on any job vacancies that existed in the area.

How helpful was the National Insurance Act?

Absence from work for illness was the major cause of poverty, therefore any money coming in as 'sick pay insurance benefit' would help a family during hard times, but the new law was limited in its help.

Firstly, only the insured worker got free medical treatment from a doctor. Other family members did not benefit from the scheme, no matter how sick they were. Nor did the scheme apply to the self-employed or the slightly better paid, or to treatment by dentists or opticians.

The limited time in which benefits were paid was a difficulty and the Government attempted to improve the scheme by abolishing the reduced benefits for the second thirteen-week period in favour of the full benefit for a period of 26 weeks. This was an improvement, but many workers were sick for longer than this.

Finally, the fact that this scheme was self-contributory reduced its success. The weekly contributions of four pennies (about two pence today) was in effect a wage cut which might have made poverty worse for many families.

Helping the unemployed

William Beveridge, an advisor to Lloyd George, argued forcibly that 'the problem of unemployment lies at the root of most other social problems.'

The National Insurance Act Part 2 tried to ease the problem of temporary unemployment, but unlike Part 1 of the Act which dealt with health insurance for all workers, Part 2 only covered unemployment for some workers in some industries, specifically building and construction, shipbuilding, mechanical engineering, iron founding, and construction of vehicles. These industries were thought to be most liable to varying employment levels at different times of the year.

In effect, unemployment insurance only covered 2.25 million workers and, like Part 1 of the Act, required contributions from workers, employers and the government. In 1912, Beveridge described how the system operated:

> 66 *Every worker in those trades had to have an unemployment booklet. Each week the employer had to attach an insurance stamp which cost 5 pence. Half of that amount (2 1/2 pence) was deducted from the worker's wages. The government also contributed 2 1/2 pence per worker. The benefit was 7 shillings a week up to a maximum of fifteen weeks. The worker claimed and received benefit at an unemployment exchange. He proved his unemployment and his capacity to work by signing an unemployment register there in working hours daily.*

Was the scheme helpful?

The help provided by this scheme was useful to the worker, as it meant they were not immediately poor if they became unemployed. With fifteen weeks to look for work, there was a good chance the worker would not face a long time without income. The new Labour Exchanges also made it much easier to find new work.

On the other hand, while in work, insured workers had an enforced pay cut as their contributions bit into weekly wages. They were only insured for fifteen weeks, which meant after this period they would have no financial support even if hit by long-term unemployment. Workers who were already poor when this scheme was introduced were not helped by it. There was no difference between a married or single worker. Rather, a worker was maintained in poverty, suffered a poverty level benefit if unemployed, then after fifteen weeks faced no help at all. And for most workers, no unemployment insurance scheme existed.

The system rested on the assumption that unemployment levels would never rise above five per cent of the workforce. This meant that contributions from those in work would easily cover the benefit paid out to those unemployed. That is what Beveridge meant by describing the system as self financing. But could the system survive if unemployment never fell below ten per cent, as happened after the First World War?

Working conditions

It can be argued that the Liberal Government's reforms were a direct result of a determination among certain Liberal ministers, such as Lloyd George and Winston Churchill, to prevent the working classes from supporting the new Labour Party. This is particularly true of the reforms to improve working conditions, but again there were serious limitations in what was achieved.

In 1906 the Liberals extended an earlier Workman's Compensation Act to cover a further 6 million workers who could now claim compensation for injuries and diseases that were the result of working conditions. However, in many trades and industries the Government failed to establish minimum wage levels or a limit to working hours, thereby doing little to ease poverty for many workers.

On the other hand, some reforms had a considerable positive impact. In 1908, miners secured an eight hour working day, the first time the length of the working day was fixed for adult men. In 1909, the Trade Boards Act tried to protect workers in the sweated trades like tailoring and lace making by setting up trade boards to fix minimum wages in jobs where workers were liable to exploitation and where trade unions could not protect them.

Two years later, in 1911, a Shops Act limited working hours for shop assistants and guaranteed a half day closing.

The introduction of Labour Exchanges in 1909 has been welcomed by some historians as a genuine attempt to help workers find jobs and minimise their time out of work. Labour Exchanges, similar to modern job centres, opened all over the country where the unemployed could register and employers with vacancies could enquire about suitable workers. Other historians, however, argue that the introduction of Labour Exchanges was ineffective. Work was still very hard to find and wages were low, thereby perhaps helping a worker to find a different low paid job but in the longer term doing little to pull them over the poverty line.

How effective were the Liberal reforms?

The Liberal reforms eased the problem of poverty for the young, sick, unemployed and old. They also attempted to improve the treatment of workers with the introduction of limited working hours and minimum wages in some industries. It can also be argued that the reforms were as successful as they could have been under the circumstances and given the scale of the poverty problem facing the Government when it came to power. It is also the case that the Liberals were distracted by the increasing threat from Germany and the expense of preparing for war, especially the naval race. Finally, the Liberals also had to deal with a mainly Conservative House of Lords which regularly opposed Liberal proposals.

On the other hand, the reforms had serious limitations. At a time when inflation was reducing the purchasing power of worker's wages and job insecurity was rising, many workers were unimpressed by the reforms. The fact that aspects of poverty such as housing were not dealt with by Liberal legislation added to the idea that the reforms 'missed their target' and were not entirely successful in dealing with poverty and need.

Perhaps the best overall comment on the Liberal reforms is that they were very successful at dealing with the situation when considering the huge task they undertook, not just in terms of the poverty of the nation but the need to change attitudes about government's role in society.

Source 4.5

This photograph was taken in 1913. The Liberals had done nothing to improve housing and slum housing seemed set to continue long after the Great War.

It is certainly true that the Liberal reforms marked a change away from 'laissez faire' to a more interventionist approach, which meant the Government took on some responsibility for the welfare of everyone in the nation. But it would be wrong to say the Liberals created a Welfare State. The Liberal reforms marked a transition point, a half way house between old 'laissez faire' attitudes and what was later called the Welfare State. Between the years of 1906 and 1914, the Liberal Government laid the foundations of a welfare state and Winston Churchill neatly summed up the nature of the Liberal reforms:

> *If we see a drowning man we do not drag him to the shore. Instead, we provide help to allow him to swim ashore.*
>
> Winston Churchill

In other words, the Liberals provided some help for the 'deserving poor' in order that they could help themselves.

Activities

1   Design a chart for each of the four main social groups helped by the Liberals.

Your four charts must clearly show the following things:

- Who was the reform meant to help?

- What was it called?

- What did the reform do?

On a scale of 1 point for very little help and 5 for very helpful, give each reform a score.

Now provide AT LEAST TWO reasons for your choice of scores.

2   You are a researcher working for the Liberal Party just after their election victory in 1906. You have been asked to prepare a report recommending whether or not the party should consider a programme of social reforms.

In your report you should:

- recommend whether or not a programme of social reforms should go ahead

- provide arguments to support your conclusions

- identify and comment on any arguments which may be presented by those who oppose your recommendation.

In your report you must use extensive background knowledge about poverty and attitudes towards poverty in late nineteenth and early twentieth-century Britain.

You may be requested to present your report in written form or as a spoken presentation lasting between two and four minutes.

Essay Writing

How successfully did the Liberal Government deal with the problem of poverty in Britain between 1906 and 1914?

Tips:

This essay is about the Liberal reforms and there are a few main themes that must be in your essay.

- You must show detailed knowledge of the Liberal reforms.

- You should organise your information into sections such as old, young, sick and unemployed.

- You must be able to explain how each reform tried to ease the problem of poverty.

- You must be able to explain the pluses and minuses of each reform.

- You must make decisions based on the information you have given about the effectiveness of each reform.

Remember your **introduction** should make clear how you intend to answer the question and what main points you will make.

Your **development** paragraphs should show off your knowledge of the Liberal reforms and you must also make comments about the success of each reform.

Your **conclusion** must answer the question asked.

The following ideas might help you do that:

- Did the Liberals solve the problem of poverty? No, but was that the intention of the reforms? No. The intention was to help sections of the deserving poor.

- The Liberals were at a transitional time in attitudes towards government help for the poor. What more could they have done? What limitations were placed on the Government by other concerns and demands for spending?

By using these ideas you should aim to reach a balanced conclusion that directly answers the main question asked.

How well did Labour deal with social problems after the Second World War?

Between 1945 and 1951 the new Labour Government passed social reforms which established a welfare state in Britain. For the first time the government took responsibility for the wellbeing of its citizens 'from the cradle to the grave'.

The experience of war between 1939 and 1945 had created a feeling in the population that 'post-war had to be better than pre-war'. During the war, cinemas showed government information films that promoted the idea of a new Britain after the war. In the words of one such film, *The Dawn Guard,* made in 1941, 'there must be no going back to the lines of men looking for work and no back to back housing with no toilets neither'. The films had two main purposes. Firstly, they made the people of Britain feel the difficulties created by war were worth enduring. Secondly, they encouraged a public debate about what Britain should be like after the war.

As the General Election of August 1945 approached, Labour issued their manifesto – their vision of what a post-war Britain would look like. It was entitled 'Let us face the future' and has been described as a 'peaceful revolution'.

However, some historians believe that Labour's promises for the future were heavily based on the achievements of previous governments, especially the Liberals of 1906–1914, the National Government of the 1930s and the wartime coalition government between 1940 and 1945. Those who support this point of view describe Labour's achievements as evolutionary, rather than revolutionary, because they grew out of – or evolved from – earlier reforms.

Source 5.1

'Post-war had to be better than pre-war.' That feeling caused many people to vote Labour in the hope that, having won the war, the people of Britain would reap the benefits of a brighter future. Why would they think Labour would deliver that?

HELP THEM FINISH THEIR JOB!
Give them homes and work!
VOTE LABOUR

Source 5.2

Clement Attlee was leader of the Labour Party and became Prime Minster in 1945.

What welfare help existed before 1945?

The Labour Government came to power in 1945, led by Clement Attlee. It is often credited with establishing a welfare state 'from cradle to grave' in Britain, where all citizens were provided with a 'safety net' of support through which none should fall into poverty. However, even before war broke out in 1939, Britain had an established network of welfare help aimed at assisting those in need. National Insurance schemes, started in 1911 and adapted later, covered most manual workers. The long term unemployed could expect some level of help from the Unemployment Assistance Boards set up in the 1930s. Government-funded schools were in every town and village and before war broke out millions of children received free milk in school.

On the other hand, it would not be fair to suggest a welfare state for all existed before 1939. Government-funded benefits were not available for all and the level of support varied from place to place across Britain. State help was only intended for the poorest sections of the community and those people above the basic level of need were still expected to pay their doctor's bills, save for their old age and pay the cost of their children's education. Mary McNeil, a 21 year old when war broke out, remembers how it was a common wedding present to have all teeth extracted by a dentist whether they were decayed or not. She said, 'now I wouldn't have to worry about toothache or paying dentist bills when we didn't have much money as young marrieds'. (From the author's private collection.)

There is a good argument in the claim that the experience of the Second World War paved the way for the later social reforms and the establishment of a welfare state. The Government organised the rationing of food, clothing and fuel and gave extra milk and meals to expectant mothers and children. Evacuation of poor children from inner city areas to the suburbs alerted the middle classes of Britain to the real poverty that still existed in the industrial slums. The bombing of cities created vast areas that had to be rebuilt while free hospital treatment for war wounded, including injured civilians, and free immunisation are examples of the move towards a national health service. To pay for these services the public got used to very high taxation levels with half of every wage packet vanishing as tax to pay for the increased government spending.

Why was the Beveridge Report important?

In late 1942, a battle was fought in the North African deserts. Its name was El Alamein and it was hugely important. For the first time a British Army had inflicted a heavy defeat on Nazi forces and although years of war stretched ahead, British people began to realise the war was winnable and they looked ahead to what a new post-war Britain might be like.

Even official announcements from the Government promoted the idea that post-war could and would be better than pre-war. A Ministry of Health statement referred to 'increasing thought for the future' and that there could be 'no return to the pre-war position...'

Although several plans were suggested for 'social reconstruction' after the war, the most important was the Beveridge Report, published in 1942. The Report identified five main causes of hardship and poverty. Beveridge called them 'the Five Giants' blocking the path to progress. These giants were:

- WANT (poverty)
- DISEASE (bad health)
- SQUALOR (bad housing)
- IGNORANCE (poor education)
- IDLENESS (unemployment)

Source 5.3

The Beveridge Report identified five giant social problems facing Britain in 1945. This cartoon shows the giant, in this case the demon 'Want', being confronted by fairy godmother Beveridge.

TRANSFORMATION SCENE
"Avaunt, foul sprite! and be no longer seen
I'll have you know I am the Fairy Queen!"

The main aim of the Report was the abolition of 'Want'. Beveridge proposed a scheme of social insurance that would guarantee help for everyone in the event of sickness, unemployment or any other difficulty which resulted in loss of income. Beveridge also argued that his social insurance plan could only succeed as part of a comprehensive social policy which included family allowances, a national health service and the prevention of mass unemployment. In other words, Beveridge argued that all five giants must be defeated if his Report was to be successful.

Beveridge said 'this is a time for revolution not for patching' and he proposed a universal welfare plan that should cover the whole population of the country. The benefits to be paid out were a right, not a charity or based on a means test. The means test had been used in the 1930s. It was a hated investigation into a family's income and any savings put aside 'for a rainy day' when assessing the amount of help a family should receive. Many unemployed workers felt stripped of their dignity by the process and it seemed that those who had struggled to save were punished by getting less help. Now Beveridge promised to get rid of such means tests.

Even before 1945 there was agreement between parties that welfare reform was needed so children could grow up free from poverty.

Even before Labour won the 1945 election, the coalition Government of wartime Britain had accepted the main ideas of the Beveridge Report as a way forward. It accepted Beveridge's plan for a unified and universal scheme and committed itself to the creation of a comprehensive National Health Service free at the point of treatment. The Family Allowances Act of 1945, a coalition measure, introduced a child allowance of five shillings a week (25 pence) for the second and all subsequent children, regardless of family income.

The wartime coalition was also concerned that there should be no return to high levels of unemployment and a White Paper on employment policy, published in 1944, accepted that future governments should maintain a 'high and stable level of employment'.

Turning to education, Beveridge had little to suggest, despite identifying ignorance as a giant. Nevertheless, even before Labour won the election, the 1944 Education Act stated that all children over the age of eleven should receive a separate secondary education free of charge and that the school-leaving age was to be raised to fifteen as soon as possible.

In conclusion, many social reforms were either in place or proposed long before Labour swept to power and claimed to establish a Welfare State. On the other hand, the Labour Party conference of 1942, which met before the Beveridge Report came out, committed a future Labour Government to a comprehensive social security scheme, family allowances and a National Health Service. So the debate about the influence of the Labour Party in the development of the welfare state after 1945 continues!

What did the Labour Government do?

Helping the poor

In his report, Beveridge had identified 'Want', or poverty, as the main giant social problem to overcome. To do that, the 1946 **National Insurance Act** created the structure of the Welfare State. It extended the original 1911 National Insurance Act to cover all adults and also put into operation a comprehensive National Health Service, effective from 5 July 1948. The Act created a compulsory contributory scheme for every worker. In return for the weekly contribution from the worker, employer and the government, an individual was entitled to sickness and unemployment benefit, an old age pension (for women at 60 and men at 65), widows' and orphans' pensions, and maternity and death grants. James Griffiths, the Minister of National Insurance, described the national insurance scheme as 'the best and cheapest insurance policy offered to…any people anywhere' (quoted on www.spartacus.schoolnet.co.uk/insurance1946.htm). However, weekly contributions took up about five per cent of average earnings and people joining the insurance scheme for the first time were not entitled to full pension benefits for ten years. The pensions themselves were still not enough to live on. By 1948 their value had been reduced by inflation. Pension levels remained below basic subsistence levels.

But what about those people not in work or who had not paid enough contributions to qualify for full benefit? A **National Assistance Act** (1948) helped them. People in need could apply for further assistance from National Assistance Boards. This was a break from the past because although applicants were 'means tested', the money for the extra assistance was provided by the Government from taxation and was not a matter for local administration. Central government even went further in asserting their influence by requiring local authorities to provide homes and other welfare services for the elderly and handicapped. Together with the National Insurance Act, this measure provided a whole new social security structure and provided a safety net through which no person should fall into serious poverty. In this case, the Labour Government really did arrange to look after the welfare of the people.

A **Family Allowance Act** (1945) was also passed to attack household poverty, although this had been started by the wartime Government. A small amount of money was paid to all mothers of two or more children. There was no attempt to 'target' the money by means tests and, significantly, the money was paid to mothers, not fathers,

Source 5.5

Family allowances were paid directly to mothers at post offices to ensure the money was used to benefit the children.

because it was felt they were more likely to spend the money on what the children and the household needed.

Finally, the **Industrial Injuries Act** of 1946 was a big improvement on previous legislation under which it had been difficult and expensive for a workman to prove that an injury or disability had been caused by his job. Now compensation was paid by the government, not individual employers, and all workers were covered.

Almost 50 years earlier, Seebohm Rowntree had identified old age, sickness, injury at work and unemployment as the main causes of poverty. Labour had directly attacked these problems and provided help and assurance to many, and in so doing removed the fear of falling into serious long term poverty.

Helping the sick

Even today, most people think the greatest achievement of the post-war Labour Government to be the creation of a **National Health Service**, possibly because it still exists and affects the lives of everyone.

The NHS began on 5 July 1948 and was based on three main aims:

5

How well did Labour deal with social problems after the Second World War?

Source 5.6

The NHS was hugely popular – and expensive – when it started.

YOUR HEALTH Service

HOW IT WILL WORK IN SCOTLAND

1 It would have universal access, meaning that the NHS was for everybody.

2 It would be comprehensive, meeting all demands and treating all medical problems.

3 It was free at point of use. No patient would be asked to pay for any treatment. In reality, of course, the service was, and is, paid for by taxation and the National Insurance payments made by every worker.

Before 5 July 1948, most health care had to be paid for. About half the male workforce was entitled to assistance through various insurance schemes, although their wives and families did not qualify. Many families had no such insurance and in times of illness had to rely for support on friends and neighbours or local charities.

The NHS offered free health care at the point of need. It entitled everybody, free of charge, to medical care from GPs, specialists and dentists. It also provided spectacles, false teeth, and maternity and child welfare services.

At first there was opposition to the scheme from doctors who resented, as they said, 'being treated like civil servants' and 90 per cent of the members of the British Medical Association threatened to boycott the new scheme.

Minister of Health Aneurin Bevan defused the situation with a new method of payments to doctors with the result that, when the NHS started on 5 July, 90 per cent of all GPs took part.

The biggest difficulty with the NHS was, and remains, its huge cost. Demand for NHS services surprised everyone. The extent of ill health among the population had not been realised. It would soon have very serious consequences as the NHS budget rose from the £134m predicted for its establishment in 1948 to £228m in 1949 and £356m in 1950. Remember that at this time Britain was only slowly recovering from the war, with huge demands on government spending. The running expenses of the NHS were reduced slightly but only at the cost of abandoning a key principle of the NHS – in 1951 adults were charged half the cost of false teeth and spectacles. Some Labour politicians, including Bevan himself, resigned in protest at this breaking of the key principle of 'free at point of use'.

Source 5.7

Critics of the NHS claimed that the new service would be chaotic and the patient would suffer. Can you see how that is suggested in this cartoon?

In the 1970s, historians Alan Sked and Chris Cook described the NHS as an:

> almost revolutionary social innovation since it improved the quality of life of most of the British people; . . . it was soon to become the social institution of which the British would feel most proud.

Alan Sked and Chris Cook, Post-War Britain: A Political History, *1979*

On the other hand, according to Charles Webster, the official historian of the NHS, writing in the late 1980s:

> The NHS failed to improve the general medical service available to the bulk of the population. The middle classes benefited to some extent but the lower classes, especially after the introduction of the prescription charge in 1952, continued to receive an inferior service, but for a higher level of payment through taxes and direct charges.

Charles Webster, National Health Service: A Political History, *2002*

Regardless of the debate over the NHS, it remains an important symbol of the brave new world of welfare reforms launched by Labour after 1945.

Education for all

Beveridge made few direct comments about the giant 'ignorance' in his report, but he made clear his desire for an education system available to all, especially the poor, which would provide opportunities and develop talent.

Before 1939, education services varied across the country. Although elementary, or primary, education had been established for some time, the quality of secondary education was variable. Many children received no education past primary stage and poorer parents could not afford the fees that some secondary schools charged. Even if a working class child was given a scholarship to pay fees, pressure from home to leave school and bring in wages was very high. In 1935, at the age of thirteen, Alex Kerr came home very pleased with himself. He had won a scholarship to 'stay on at school', take exams and get a good job. His father spoke to him. 'He told me to get a job and bring in wages. Within the month I was working at the post office.' (From the author's private collection.)

The giant of ignorance was tackled by the **Education Act** of 1944 which took effect in Scotland in 1945. It raised the school leaving age to fifteen and all children were to get free secondary education.

Although the Education Act became law under Labour, the Labour Government can take little credit for it and it is another point in the argument that post-war social reform was not entirely the work of the Labour Government. In fact, the wartime coalition began discussing education reform in 1941. The main ideas at the foundations of educational reform were to be equality of opportunity and the creation of a system which would allow working class children to progress through school without being restricted by the demands to pay expensive fees. However, the reality of the Education Act of 1944 was rather different from its original aims.

The credit for the education reform is given to R.A. Butler. He argued that the future of Britain's strength and wealth lay in scientific and technical training so technical education should be a priority. Butler's idea was to create a three level education system of technical, grammar, and secondary modern schools. In Scotland, the last two were usually called senior and junior secondary, respectively. Butler's original idea was for each type of school to have equal status, but very soon the grammar/ senior secondary schools were seen to be the 'best', while the creation of high-quality technical schools never took root. It is argued that the influence of church people and politicians who were products of private schools killed off the idea of respected technical schools.

The desire to create a fair and socially balanced education system retreated in the face of reality. There was a small increase in the proportion of working class boys at grammar school but the real benefits lay with the middle classes. Grammar school fees were abolished and government spending on the grammar schools and senior secondaries raced ahead of the expenditure on junior secondary modern schools.

There was also concern about the use of exams at an early age to categorise children. Then and now many people opposed the idea of deciding a child's future at age eleven or twelve.

All children sat an exam at eleven (called the eleven plus exam, or the 'Qualy', short for the qualification exam, in Scotland), the results of which decided the type of secondary school a child would attend. For those who passed the eleven plus exam or 'qualy', the system worked well. They went to senior secondary schools and were expected to stay on at school after fifteen, go to university or get jobs in management and the professions.

However, those children who failed the exam went to a junior secondary. They were expected to leave school at fifteen and go into unskilled jobs. By failing the eleven plus, thousands of children were trapped in a world of low expectations and inferior education.

Butler had never intended such harsh decisions to be made about children in his original proposals but the reality of the education reforms became increasingly criticised. By the mid-1960s new thinking was moving state schools towards the comprehensive model, although that, too, has its critics.

What was done to improve housing?

In 1945, most of Britain's cities still had slum areas and overcrowding was still a serious problem, made worse by bomb damage during the war. After the two-night Clydebank blitz of 1941, for example, only seven houses out of a total stock of 12,000 remained intact. Cities across Britain suffered and as peace broke out a huge rebuilding programme was needed. Labour's manifesto recognised the need:

 Labour's pledge is firm and direct – it will proceed with a housing programme with the maximum practical speed until every family in this island has a good standard of accommodation.

Labour Party Manifesto, 1945

The government aimed to build 200,000 houses each year, but economic conditions were not helpful – raw materials were in short supply and expensive. Nevertheless, the government was successful. Although only 55,400 new houses were completed in 1946, by 1948 over 280,000 had been built; way above the government's target. Many were council houses for rent and of those many were 'factory made houses' – 'prefabs' for short – which were quickly assembled on site. Even in 1951, Labour still averaged well over 200,000 houses a year. Cities became encircled with council-owned housing estates providing quality new homes for those people moving from the inner cities. These homes were in many ways better than the overcrowded tenements left behind. On the plus side, the houses had a separate kitchen, bedrooms and a living room. There was gas and electric power, hot and cold

Source 5.8

Labour built new prefabricated houses on the outskirts of cities. Why were they called 'prefabs'?

water, indoor toilets in a bathroom and in the 1950s most houses were two stories high, usually with gardens front and back. The down side was summed up by Alex Kerr, who moved from central Edinburgh to a council estate on the south side in the early 1950s:

> *I was far from my work, my friends and the town. I had to walk 2 miles to the nearest bus stop. The tar was still wet on the roads, there were cows in the fields behind us and when I came home from work there was just the tele, my wife and son. No pubs, no cinemas, not even shops at first. A chip van came round on Friday night. But all the neighbours were in it together. We soon made new friends.*
>
> From the author's private collection

Overall, the new council estates were a saviour for people living in crowded tenements in the centres of Scotland's cities. Not least among the advantages was the council's role as a major landlord which protected people from unfair exploitation by private landlords. In the 1950s, council rent was one third of that in the private sector.

Unfortunately, nobody had foreseen the huge demand for housing after the war. The increase in marriages, the rapid increase in the birth rate and the reluctance of families to continue living as extended families in cramped conditions all combined to swallow up houses as fast as they were built. Newspaper stories of families 'squatting' in disused army camps while they waited for housing, as at Duddingston in Edinburgh, all added to the impression that Labour had failed in their promise. In spite of Labour's undoubted achievement given the difficult economic situation, there was still a serious housing shortage in 1951 and long waiting lists for council housing.

The **New Towns Act** in 1946 laid the plans for fourteen New Towns to be built, including Glenrothes and East Kilbride. These were to be 'people-friendly' towns to relieve the housing problems in older cities.

As part of the vision of a new Britain, and also to provide space for the increase in house building, the New Towns Act gave the Government the power to decide where new towns should be built and to set up development corporations to carry out the projects. The aim was to create towns that were healthy and pleasant to live in as well as being geared to the needs of the townspeople, unlike the uncontrolled growth of Britain's nineteenth-century industrial cities. In Scotland, East Kilbride and Glenrothes are examples of post-war new towns. Livingston also reflects the vision of the New Towns Act, although it did not grow until the 1960s. Altogether fourteen new towns were established in Britain before the end of the Labour Government in 1951.

Source 5.9

New Towns were an idealistic hope for a bright new future. Did they live up to the dream?

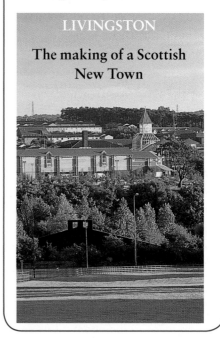

LIVINGSTON

The making of a Scottish New Town

Jobs for all?

The traditional view of post-war employment levels is that all governments from 1945 until the 1970s were committed to a policy of full employment, which meant that everyone who wanted a job could get one. In 1944, a 'White Paper' (government proposal for discussion) seemed to accept the need to aim for 'full employment' and the Labour Manifesto of 1945 made its policy clear, while at the same time raising doubts about the commitment of the other parties to achieving the goal of 'full' employment:

> 66 *All parties pay lip service to the idea of jobs for all. Where agreement ceases is in the degree of control of private industry that is necessary to achieve the desired end. Our opponents say, "Full employment. Yes! If we can get it without interfering too much with private industry." We say, "Full employment in any case, and if we need to keep a firm public hand on industry in order to get jobs for all, very well. No more dole queues, in order to let the Bosses of Big Business remain kings in their own castles. The price of so-called "economic freedom" for the few is too high if it is bought at the cost of idleness and misery for millions. There must be no depressed areas in the New Britain.*

Labour Party Manifesto, 1945

Labour's answer to the problem of unemployment was **nationalisation**. The policy of nationalisation had its roots in Labour's socialist beliefs and was adopted as party policy after the First World War. In theory, nationalisation meant that the government would take over major industries and run them for the benefit of the country rather than the private owners. Profits would be used by the government rather than filling the pockets of private owners and in this way Labour believed they could control and manage the economy more effectively and maintain full employment.

However, revisionist historians now take a different view of Labour's policy and wonder just how responsible the government was for maintaining the goal of 'jobs for all'. When the Labour Government began in 1945 there was a private expectation that unemployment figures would level out at about eight per cent. That was still a high number of people out of work, but to the Government's surprise unemployment levels tumbled to 'full employment'. What caused this? Quite simply, the boom in private investment and building after 1945 was the main reason. The need to recover and rebuild after the war soaked up workers and Labour took the credit for reducing unemployment.

5

How well did Labour deal with social problems after the Second World War?

Source 5.10

Nationalisation was an attempt by the government to control and manage the economy so that high unemployment could be avoided.

THIS COLLIERY IS NOW MANAGED BY THE ~~N~~ATIONAL ~~C~~OAL BOARD ~~O~~N BEHALF OF THE PEOPLE JANUARY 1ST 1947

How successful was the Labour Government of 1945–1951?

Labour did try to 'deliver' its manifesto promises despite serious problems right from the beginning. Victory in the Second World War bankrupted Britain and critics have pointed out that Britain was therefore in no position to launch a welfare programme. They argue that the Government should have directed resources towards industrial reconstruction first to strengthen Britain's economy. In *The Audit of War: The Illusion and Reality of Britain as a Great Nation* (1986), Correlli Barnett argued that Labour's first priority should have been re-equipping industry and the development of technical education. Even Labour's own 1945 manifesto recognised the problem:

> 66 *But great national programmes of education, health and social services are costly things. There is no good reason why Britain should not afford such programmes, but she will need full employment and the highest possible industrial efficiency in order to do so.*
>
> *Correlli Barnett,* The Audit of War: The Illusion and Reality of Britain as a Great Nation, *2001*

Instead, the Labour Government focused on their attempt to build a fair society in Britain where help was available to all – often referred to as the 'New Jerusalem' of the welfare state. Barnett reminds readers that a central point of earlier social reform had been to increase national efficiency (remember the Liberal reforms?), yet Labour seemed to forget or ignore this point. Barnett asked how far Labour's welfare reforms equipped the nation to compete against other nations.

Developing Barnett's ideas further, Professor Jose Harris, in his book *William Beveridge: A Biography* (1997), has shown that while most countries in Western Europe increased their social spending after 1945, other countries targeted their social spending on the labour force, with the aim of increasing industrial efficiency. In Britain, spending was more generous towards the old, the sick and the poor, which had no direct economic benefit.

However, it would be wrong to criticise Beveridge, and the Labour administration between 1945 and 1951, for what they did not do. In the words of Sir Keith Berrill, a senior Treasury official, 'We had won the War and we voted ourselves a nice peace.'

Critics have argued that the government was either doing too much for the people – leading towards the modern cliché of 'a nanny state' – or not enough, and that the Beveridge Report was a lost opportunity to build a better Britain. But these critics miss the point. The Beveridge Report provided a beacon of hope to war-weary people who wanted to believe that post-war Britain would be a land worth fighting for. Labour's reforms went a long way to create a post-war Britain based on ideas of fairness and

Source 5.11

By 1951, Labour was criticised for not delivering all their promises. This poster tried to win back those who had voted Labour in 1945.

help for all who needed it. The living standards of the poor were raised and people looked forward to a time of increasing opportunity and prosperity. In the 1950s, Conservative Prime Minister Harold Macmillan told the British people they had 'never had it so good'.

The prosperity and feel-good factor of the 1950s had its roots in the improvements and reforms put into practice by Labour. By 1951, the Labour Government had achieved a transformation of British society in a way that improved the lives of millions of people, male and female, young and old. For the first time the financial uncertainties of unemployment and serious illness were banished by the Welfare State, and a start had been made to provide decent housing and education for everyone.

Source 5.12

Labour lost the 1951 election. They failed to build on the huge package of reforms they passed between 1945 and 1951. This Labour poster makes no mention of their successes and can only play on old fears from the 1930s. Labour seemed to have run out of ideas.

Activities

1   Work in pairs or groups of three, maximum.

The design
Design THREE word searches, each one no larger than ten squares by ten squares.

One of your puzzles must contain only words or phrases linked to the main themes or issues in this chapter, e.g. welfare.

Your second puzzle must contain only words or phrases linked to the actions of the Labour Government. Your puzzle must contain eight words or phrases which are vital to any coverage of this topic – for example, National Assistance – and which are used within this chapter.

Your third puzzle must contain only names of significant people in this chapter, e.g. Beveridge.

The solution
The words/phrases can go in any direction and phrases can be split.

Each word/phrase must have a definition or clue to help someone find them.

When you have completed your puzzles, exchange them with another group and find the answers to the puzzles you receive. **continued** ➡

How well did Labour deal with social problems after the Second World War?

Activities *continued*

2 This activity is similar to the one outlined at the end of Chapter 1, when you were provided with a partly completed spider diagram illustrating the main themes in the section and the details attached to each theme.

This time you must complete the whole diagram yourself.

Draw a spider diagram around the central question 'How did Labour tackle the social problems facing Britain between 1945 and 1951?'

Around your central question, draw five boxes. Each box should contain ONE of Beveridge's five giants. From each of the boxes, draw at least three more legs, each one leading to a particular Labour reform which tried to tackle the social problem identified in the box. Draw a fourth leg from each of the giant reforms to include a brief assessment comment on Labour's success or failure.

Do that for all five of the giants. When you have finished you have the information needed to describe and assess what Labour did about each of the social problems identified by Beveridge.

Sample Essay Questions

1 How successfully did the Labour Government deal with the social problems facing Britain at the end of the Second World War?

2 To what extent did the Labour Government of 1945 to 1951 defeat the giant problems identified in the Beveridge Report?

You are now at the end of this course.

You now have all the skills needed to remind yourself of what makes a good essay and the three areas that will gain you marks. Apply the PROCESS of essay writing to the titles on this page.

Germany

Contents

Why did nationalism grow in the German states after 1815?

> 'Allons enfants de la Patrie
>
> Le jour du gloire est arrivé!'
>
> [Arise children of the fatherland
>
> The day of glory has arrived!]
>
> With these words ringing in their ears, the soldiers of France unleashed a quarter century of war on Europe. During this time, old forms of government were swept aside, new national areas were created and the ideas of nationalism and liberalism were carried across Europe. With the defeat of Napoleon I in 1815, the leaders of 'old' Europe tried to turn back the clock. However, it was not easy to put the genies of nationalism and liberalism back into the lamp!

Germany after the Napoleonic Wars

Prior to the French Revolutionary and Napoleonic Wars, the Holy Roman Empire had occupied much of central Europe and many of the German states had been part of that. Napoleon had reorganised the ramshackle structure into the Confederation of the Rhine. This, on the surface at least, resembled a more modern German state. Over 400 'German' states had been swept into an organisation comprising just 16. However, the allies who met at Vienna were determined to rid Europe of as much of Napoleon's legacy as possible, and thus the Confederation of the Rhine was unacceptable. Nonetheless, this organisation had provided the 'German people' with their first taste of a national German state and the idea inspired writers, thinkers and eventually the German people themselves to seek a single German state.

What factors favoured the unification of Germany in 1815?

The main unifying force was language. Although dialects were common, there were about 25 million people who spoke the same language and who shared the same culture and literature. Thus, it used to be said that:

> *France ruled the continent; Britain ruled the waves; whilst Germany ruled the clouds.*

Source 6.1

Areas where German was the principal language.

The people speaking this language occupied a belt of territory that dominated the middle of Europe, though there were areas of German speakers in Denmark and lands occupied by Russia. There was therefore a rough geographical idea of where the German states lay.

Who wanted a powerful and united Germany?

One group that supported the idea of a united Germany was the writers and thinkers of the eighteenth century. Men such as Heinrich Heine and Johann Fichte had encouraged German consciousness.

In *Reden an die deutsche Nation* (Address to the German Nation), Fichte wrote:

> " *The separation of the Germans from the other European nations is based on Nature. Through a common language and through common national characteristics which unite the Germans, they are separate from the others… Those who speak the same language are joined to each other by a multitude of invisible bonds…they understand each other and have the power to make themselves understood more and more clearly; they belong to one another and are by nature one and inseparably whole.*

> Quoted in Ian Mitchell, Bismarck and the Development of Germany, *1980*

Fichte also believed that Germany had to unite for economic reasons. The industrialisation of Britain, and later France, had left the German states at a disadvantage. German businessmen wanted an end to trade barriers

Why did nationalism grow in the German states after 1815?

between the German states in the *Bund*, and they wanted to be able to exploit all of the natural resources scattered amongst the various states. Economists such as List also believed the governments of the German states should help the development of 'German' industries by imposing tariffs on competition from abroad. There was also support for a railway system for the German-speaking area. Those changes, if they happened, would help accelerate progress towards a united Germany. Such views won widespread support amongst the intellectual middle classes and industrial businessmen.

As T.S. Hamerow noted:

> 66 *The liberal creed derived its economic support from manufacturers, bankers, entrepreneurs…but its intellectual defenders generally came from the ranks of the learned professions.*

Quoted in *Ian Mitchell,* Bismarck and the Development of Germany, *1980*

Nationalist feelings were first expressed among students and the great German writers and poets.

Source 6.2

Student demonstration at Hambacherfest in the 1830s.

> 66 *Even in 1815 there were tens of thousands of people, especially among the young, the educated, and the middle and upper classes, who felt passionately that Germans deserved to have a fatherland in the same way as the English and the French already had.*

Andrina Stiles, The Unification of Germany, *1989*

Part of the reason for this was the means by which the rulers of the old European states had inspired their people to rise up to defeat the French enemy. The people of central Europe had been encouraged by their leaders to take part in a nationalist rebellion against the French invaders. But these nationalist hopes were ignored by the peacemakers at Vienna. The failure of this meeting to encourage any nationalist hopes was an important reason for the support of nationalist causes after 1815.

Following 1815, nationalist feelings were first expressed in the universities and amongst Germany's great writers and poets. During the wars, the universities had witnessed the emergence of nationalist student societies called *Burschenschaften*. These were dedicated to seeing the French driven from German soil and had grown since 'Germany's' success in the Battle of the Nations (or Battle of Leipzig) in 1813. However, their nationalist enthusiasm tended to be of the romantic kind, passionate yet with no clear idea as to how their aims might be achieved.

It could be argued that these supporters of the nationalist cause were merely following in the footsteps of earlier eighteenth-century writers. Wilhelm von Humboldt had already inspired the nationalist cause with his demands for the restriction of the power of the monarch. Poets like Goethe also praised the idea of the nation-state. The folk tales of the Brothers Grimm celebrated Germany's past and looked forward to the day when it would at last be united in an independent nation. Their studies indicated that the German language had come from a common source. United by language, it was felt that the Germans should also be united politically. An example of the extremes to which members of these student groups would go was provided in 1819 when an agent of the Tsar called Kotzebu was murdered to show that tyranny would not be tolerated in 'Germany'. Needless to say the authorities used this as an excuse to crack down on such organisations by using the Carlsbad Decrees of 1819.

But to what extent did Nationalist ideas filter down to the ordinary German citizen?

German historians have often called this period *Vormärz* (pre-March) since they regard such restrictions as part of the background causes of the Year of Revolutions in 1848. Much of the debate in these societies was theoretical in nature and probably above the understanding of the ordinary Germans. Evidence does exist to show that workers, now increasingly huddled together in large urban areas, were beginning to take a real interest in politics and philosophy but only in relatively small numbers. Thus, as Andrina Stiles comments, 'Liberalism and nationalism remained largely middle-class before 1848'.

Nonetheless, following news of revolution in Paris in 1830, there was another wave of student activity within the German states. At the Hambach festival the red, gold and black colours were first used to symbolise German nationalism. Although such activities and demonstrations did little to advance the cause of German unification, they did show that, beneath the surface, nationalist sentiment was never far away.

This was clearly demonstrated in 1840 when France threatened to extend its eastern frontier with the German Confederation to the natural boundary of the Rhine. Germany itself seemed to be threatened and forces, hostile to the French, were rapidly mobilised. What was significant about this was that these forces were not confined to the parts of the Rhineland that would be absorbed, nor were they limited to Prussia whose land this now was, nor were they restricted to the middle classes. For the first time since liberation from Napoleon, ordinary Germans were roused to the defence of the fatherland. The events of 1840 showed that nationalist feeling had spread to large numbers of ordinary German citizens. For its stout defence of the Rhine, Prussia emerged with great credit amongst German nationalists.

Certainly, as industrialisation and urbanisation increased, evidence does exist to show that workers were taking an interest in politics, but only in relatively small numbers.

Industrialisation and population changes

It was in the area of economics that the German states first experienced the benefits of some form of unity. The early nineteenth century was a time of great change within all European states. Indeed it has been suggested that the political changes of the nineteenth century can only be explained by an understanding of the social and economic developments of the time. David Thomson has noted that:

 No social and political order could have remained unaffected by so immense an increase in humanity. And the events of the nineteenth century remain unintelligible unless the greatest revolution of all is kept constantly in mind.

David Thomson, Europe since Napoleon, 1965

The population of Europe grew rapidly in this period. This increase in numbers led to industrialisation and the drift of country folk to the towns, looking for new employment opportunities and, hopefully, better working and living conditions. The twin forces of urbanisation and industrialisation were important factors leading to change. In the German states, the population increased from 25 million in 1816 to over 34 million by 1840. However, it is necessary to keep the scale of these changes in mind. In the

1840 census, only 600,000 out of a population of 34 million were classed as factory workers. Nonetheless, it has been argued that the forces unleashed by industrialisation did help push the German states towards unification. Ian Mitchell suggests that the political fragmentation of the German states was the most important obstacle to the economic development of Germany.

Source 6.3

Growth of industry in Germany prior to 1848.

Mitchell points to the existence of many different currencies, customs regulations, taxes and legal systems as examples of the problems German businessmen faced. Thus, it is no surprise to find middle class businessmen at the forefront of demands for a more united market to enable them to compete with countries such as Britain.

	Coal production (million tonnes)		Pig iron production (thousand tonnes)	
Period	German States	Britain	German States	Britain
1820s	1.6	22.3	90	669
1830s	3.0	28.1	146	1142
1840s	6.1	48.6	184	1786

The effect of Prussian economic expansion

With Prussia's acquisition of land on the River Rhine after 1815, its territory spread across northern Germany. Prussia's control over the Rhineland, many miles away from her main territory, meant that it had good reason to try to reach an agreement with its neighbours to ensure

relatively free travel of goods and people between its lands in the east and west. Complaints about the burden of taxes levied as goods were moved across the German states prompted the Prussian authorities to abolish all internal taxes within Prussia itself in 1818, creating a large free trade area. Ironically, they were able to take advantage of the good road network that had been set up during the period of French occupation, and wished to see this extended. Taxes were put on goods entering Prussia and these were used to improve communications which helped meet the needs of businessmen. Prussia's control of the great rivers of the Rhine and the Elbe encouraged other German states to realise they should reach agreements with Prussia. In 1834, the *Zollverein* (Customs Union) was established and two years later 25 of the 39 German states had signed up to this new economic free-trade area. Significantly, Austria was excluded from this development.

As William Carr commented:

 Certainly Prussia was not thinking in terms of political unification when it founded the Customs Union. Nor had the states joined it out of love for Prussia but simply and solely to escape from the financial and economic difficulties that beset them.

It would be inappropriate to see the Zollverein as the forerunner of German political unity. There is ample evidence to show that Prussia did not have it all its own way in the union and many of the members refused to be bullied by Prussia into taking its lead or advice.

William Carr, A History of Germany, 1969

The effect of continued German economic and industrial growth

Further developments in the 1830s and 1840s pushed the German states into closer co-operation. The development of the railways from the mid-1830s had a dramatic impact upon the German states, ending their isolation from one another and enabling the transport and exploitation of Germany's natural resources. By 1850, over 3000 miles of railway had been built, with the same economic spin-offs as had been experienced elsewhere in Europe. Their development created employment opportunities in their construction phase and, later on, men were needed to run the services. Demand for coal, iron and steel all increased and the lowering of transport costs provided a boost to a host of other industries, including the cotton and woollen industries. The example of this economic co-operation between the German states provided encouragement for those seeking a political solution to the issue of German unity. As Andrina Stiles wrote in *The Unification of Germany*:

> 66 The Zollverein was a force for unity in the 1840s and therefore a focal point for nationalist sentiments. As a result Prussia, despite its reactionary political sympathies, came to be regarded by many as the natural leader of a united Germany.

Andrina Stiles, The Unification of Germany, *1990*

Source 6.4

Railways in Germany prior to 1848.

Prussia as a leader

Prussia, ruled by the Hohenzollern family, and dominated by its *Junker* (Prussian nobles) farmers, had a reputation of being ultra conservative (cautious about change) rather than a reactionary (totally against change) power. So it is perhaps surprising that nationalists and liberals looked to Berlin, the capital of Prussia, for some signs of leadership in the question of German unity.

Despite years of discussion in the 1820s and 1830s, the idea of a united Germany remained just a dream. But some changes were happening. In the states of south-west Germany support for liberals increased and in the state of

Baden half of the elected members of the lower House of Parliament were converted to liberal ideas. This was matched by demands in the state of Hesse-Darmstadt for changes in the rules governing elections.

Within Prussia, hopes for change came in 1840 when Frederick William IV became King. An unstable monarch who swung between political extremes, he first won the approval of the Liberals with his release of political prisoners, relaxation of the censorship laws and the appointment of liberal leaders to posts within the Council of State. This led to demands for a constitution for Prussia and a single parliament to help run the country. At this point Frederick William grew afraid of too much change. He abandoned his liberal ideas. When the King then restored press censorship in 1843 he won great sympathy among the *Junker* landowners. Thus, as had happened so often during this period, one step forward often resulted in two steps backwards.

Activities

1 Using the information in this chapter, write a summary of the forces in favour of nationalism in the German states as this time, explaining the reasons for that support.

Essay Writing

Your course work will be assessed in an exam which, in the case of Germany, will consist of one essay from a choice of four. This section provides some suggestions and advice on how to tackle an essay.

> **To what extent did the *Zollverein* stimulate nationalism in the German states before 1850?**

- Decide what the question is asking you to do. NB: the essay is not just about the Prussian customs union.

- The essay is about **all** the developments between 1815 and 1850 that encouraged German nationalism. It is necessary to show how each contributed and assess its importance.

- Try to show the examiner that you know about historical debate by using a quotation in support of or against the point mentioned in the title, e.g. William Carr referred to the *Zollverein* as 'the mighty lever of German unification'.

continued ➡

Essay Writing *continued*

- The conclusion should draw together the main themes. Try to reach a balanced conclusion that considers all the factors leading to the growth of nationalism. Mention the differences in progress between them. Finally, make clear what side of the argument you support. Was German nationalism due to economic developments?

How much had German nationalism grown by 1850?

When the representatives of the victorious powers from the Napoleonic Wars signed the Treaty of Vienna in 1815, they might have been forgiven for thinking that their task was complete. The traditional rulers of the European states had been restored to power and, as far as possible, the boundaries had been redrawn to turn back the clock to 1789 before the wars with France began. The twin forces of liberalism and nationalism seemed to have been defeated.

However, it was to prove impossible to prevent growing support for these twin ideas as events up until 1850 were to show.

The attitude of the middle classes

It was from amongst the educated middle classes that calls for German unity were most insistent. They were resentful of the fact that although paying most in taxes towards government expenditure, they had little say in how that money should be spent. There was also resentment over the fact that the upper classes were mainly exempt from taxation yet, at the same time, it was members of the upper classes who got the best government jobs or became officers in the army.

The middle classes were also the generators of the new wealth of the German states through trade and industry. They also provided legal and financial services, all of which were underpinning the industrialisation of many of the German states. They could see the benefits of, at the very least, economic unification which would create a larger national market. It would therefore be a natural step from this to political unification.

Liberals were also resentful of their political exclusion from government business. The restoration of the traditional rulers after 1815 saw the return of the old ruling classes and political oppression. The ideas of 'liberty, equality and fraternity', born out of the French Revolution, had inspired the Liberals to challenge their autocratic rulers. Liberals were therefore disappointed by the results of the Congress of Vienna and wished to see some restoration of political freedom and a relaxation of press censorship.

Despite these desires for greater political freedom and moves towards unification of the German states, the opponents of nationalism were to prove too powerful in the period up to 1850. The reasons for this are not difficult to work out. The old ruling class had control of the army which could be, and was, used to suppress nationalist uprisings in the 1820s and 1830s. As long as the majority of the population lived in the countryside, it was very difficult for liberal and nationalist supporters to persuade this group to support their ideals.

Attitude of the peasants

Peasants formed the largest group in German society and could have had the greatest influence on the success of the nationalist cause. However, the peasantry had to deal with more immediate problems. Faced with rising rents and harsh working conditions, peasants were leaving the countryside in increasing numbers in an attempt to earn a better living in the growing towns. As urban populations grew there was an increasing demand for food so fewer peasants in the countryside had to grow more food. The spreading agricultural revolution forced more changes in the countryside and there was great pressure for the peasants to combine their small farms into larger commercial enterprises. All of this created resentment between the rulers and the ruled.

Sources of discontent

The traditional view of the causes of the revolutionary activity is that the uprising in Paris against the rule of King Louis-Philippe had a ripple effect across the whole of continental Europe. However, this version fails to take into account the various changes that were taking place at this time and against which the traditional rulers were powerless to act. These changes included the progress of industrialisation, with all of its negative aspects – poor working conditions, exploitation of female and child labour – as well as the threat posed to independent craftsmen working from home. As a result of the decline in available work in the villages, more people were seeking homes and employment in the new urban centres, as the following table shows:

Growth of German cities

City	1800	1850	1880
Munich	30,000	110,000	230,000
Cologne	50,000	97,000	145,000
Essen	4,000	9,000	57,000
Düsseldorf	10,000	27,000	95,000

Faced with poor living conditions and high rents, working classes in the towns and cities were now much more willing to protest and demonstrate. It was much easier for potential agitators to rouse the masses of exploited

urban workers than had previously been the case. Even in the countryside, those who remained found it difficult to make a living. Landowners had been increasing rents to such an extent that many peasant farmers were on the brink of losing their livelihood.

Additionally, there was a marked decline in the amount of food available due to poor harvests in 1846 and 1847 and, as in Ireland in 1845–46, there was an outbreak of the potato blight. Potatoes were the main diet of much of the German peasantry and the outbreak of the blight had a devastating impact. Such shortages of food had happened in the past, but what made the effect even greater in 1848 was the growth of the population.

Source 7.1

The uprising in Paris against King Louis-Philippe is often blamed for spreading revolutionary activity across Europe.

People living in the towns were faced with a shortage of food and an increase in prices at a time when many of them were losing their jobs due to the recession and could not afford to pay the prices demanded. This combination of higher prices, lower wages for those in employment and widespread unemployment all combined to produce a fall in the workers' standard of living.

In both the towns and the countryside, the people were unhappy at this state of affairs and began to make demands, including a call for better housing and pay and improved working and living conditions. There were, however, no demands for political change. There was no call for democracy, liberalism or nationalism. The workers and peasants simply wanted to be able to survive from day to day and they would support any government that might improve their conditions.

It was not just the lower classes who were discontented. There were rumblings of unrest amongst the middle classes as well, for a variety of reasons. There was increasing frustration about the lack of job opportunities amongst men qualified to fill the traditional middle class jobs of medicine, the law and civil service administrators. In most cases, the senior posts were held by the younger sons of the nobility. The middle classes were angered at their lack of power and influence. The ruling classes still dominated the government and they took little heed of the new ideas of liberalism and nationalism. However, unlike the workers and peasants, middle class demands included fairer taxation, education for all and the creation of a united German Republic.

By the beginning of 1848, a combination of differing demands from the working classes, the peasants and the middle classes all had one common aim – change.

The forces of change

Source 7.2

Street battles in Berlin, 18–19 March 1848.

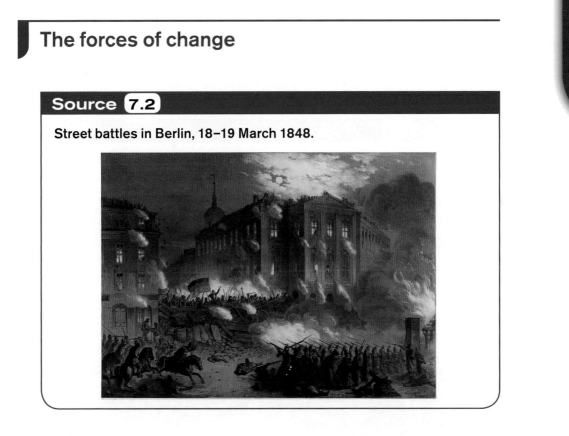

Pressure for change finally came to a head in the *Bund* in February 1848. Change seemed a real possibility and demonstrations were held in many of the German states. In Vienna, Chancellor Metternich was forced to flee the city like a common criminal. The Austrian authorities were also faced with simultaneous uprisings of ethnic minorities within the empire, notably the Hungarians and Italians. Within Prussia, there had been demonstrations in Berlin during which the army had opened fire, sparking off several days of

street fighting. It was at this point that the contradictory nature of Frederick William IV became obvious. While opposed to the demands of the demonstrators, he was shocked by the death of so many protesters. He suddenly seemed to accept their demands and even appeared wrapped in the colours of black, red and gold – the emblem of a united Germany. King Frederick William IV declared:

> 66 *To my people and to the German nation – Germany is in a state of internal ferment and can be threatened by external danger from more than one side. It can be saved from this double danger only by the most intimate unity of the German princes and peoples under one leadership. Today I take over this leadership for the days of danger… I have today taken the old German colours… Prussia henceforth merges into Germany.*
>
> Frederick William, 17 March 1848

To the nationalist and liberal revolutionaries the time seemed right. With Austria distracted by events within its empire, and Prussia appearing willing to take the lead, the creation of a united Germany might just be achieved.

Source 7.3

This painting by Gemalde von F. Sorriieu (1848) shows that the forces of nationalism were present across all of Europe.

The Frankfurt Parliament

Late in 1874 there were calls from several German states for meetings to tackle the issue of German unity. Invitations were sent to all states to be represented at the *Vorparlament* (preliminary parliament) to meet at the end of March 1848. The response was spectacular. Five hundred and

seventy four delegates met in Frankfurt and, after long debate, they agreed on a mechanism for the election of a national Constituent Assembly. This parliament would be tasked with drawing up the rules of government – or constitution – for a united Germany.

Membership of this Constituent Assembly would be based on one member for every 50,000 inhabitants and they were to be elected by appropriate means in each of the member states. Meanwhile, the old rulers of the German states agreed to the idea of an elected parliament, but they had little real sympathy for the idea of an all-German parliament. Afraid of losing their thrones, they waited and watched until they could safely re-establish their traditional control.

The Constituent Assembly was also known as the Frankfurt Parliament. It met in May 1848, but hopes for change were soon dashed. The Assembly was dominated by the educated middle classes whose real interest lay more in the creation of a united Germany than in social reform.

The assembly also lacked power and relied too much on the support of King Frederick William of Prussia. At first the King supported the parliament but then changed his mind and decided he did not want to help unite Germany. The lack of an independent armed force directly under the control of the Frankfurt Parliament was a great hindrance to the assembly, which had to rely on the Prussian army to crush the disturbances which had begun occurring throughout the German states.

Source 7.4

The Frankfurt Assembly.

In the meantime, the work of the assembly proceeded at a snail's pace. It was agreed that there was a need for a constitution but no agreement as to what it should contain. Eventually, it was decided that the parliament would consist of two parts, or Houses. The Lower House would be elected by secret ballot and all men over 25 would be able to vote.

It is easy to sympathise with the view of the English historian A.J.P. Taylor when he described the events at Frankfurt as suffering:

> " *from too much experience rather than too little; too much calculation, too much foresight, too many elaborate combinations, too much statesmanship.*
>
> A.J.P. Taylor, quoted in David Thomson, Europe Since Napoleon, 1965

Included in the constitution were freedom of speech and of worship, equality before the law and an end to discrimination based on class. These were giant steps towards a more liberal, democratic and fair German society but it had taken nine months to produce them. By the time the constitution was agreed, the moment had passed and the days of the Frankfurt Parliament were limited.

Establishing an exact definition of 'Germany' was another problem that the assembly faced. There were two points of view and arguments between supporters of each idea split the German nationalists and weakened their cause.

Grossdeutschland would include Austria and some even argued that its empire should also be included. This solution found little favour with Austria, who was less than enthusiastic about a united Germany. It was favoured by the southern German states who believed that Austria would act as a counter-balance to a Germany dominated by Prussia.

Kleindeutschland supporters wanted Austria and its empire excluded completely. Naturally, Prussia favoured this as it would lead to her dominating any new country.

Eventually, it was decided to exclude Austria but it was by no means a clear cut decision.

Vote to exclude Austria

Yes	No	Abstention	Absent	Total
261	224	3	70	558

The failure of the Assembly

By March 1849, the new Austrian Emperor Franz Josef II was firmly in control of his country once more. He was totally against the idea of Austria being absorbed into a united Germany and he sought to re-establish Austrian leadership within the *Bund* and restore Austria's total control.

Too late, the Frankfurt delegates at last decided to offer the crown of a united Germany to Frederick William of Prussia. He, too, had now firmly crushed the rebels within Prussia and had no desire to fan the flames of revolution any further. With Frederick William's rejection of the crown of a united Germany, the days of revolutionary activity were over. Delegates from Austria and other states were withdrawn and the assembly finally disintegrated.

Without clear aims, decisive leadership and an armed force to enforce its decisions, the Frankfurt Parliament had been unable to fulfil its revolutionary aims. To many, it seemed that a great opportunity to create a liberal, united Germany had been missed.

Why did the 1848 Revolutions fail?

First of all, the revolutionary leaders had no clear aims about what was to be achieved. There was no agreement on *klein-* versus *gross-deutschland* or whether Germany should have a monarchy or be a republic.

Secondly, the German rulers maintained their authority and used it to regain their power when the tide of revolution turned. They had bought time by granting reforms that allowed them to retain control and wait for better days. More importantly, they retained control of their armies. These could be used to crush any remaining revolutionaries.

Thirdly, the reforms that were granted, such as agreeing to a constitution, could be easily reversed at a later date.

Fourthly, the 'revolutionaries' were divided. Some were not even revolutionaries! Workers had been roused to action by hunger and poverty and demanded higher wages and shorter working hours. But these demands were at odds with those of the middle classes, many of whom were the employers of the workers.

Fifthly, the Frankfurt Parliament was dependent on Prussia for armed support. It had no armed force to ensure its decisions were followed.

Finally, the rulers of the 39 German states could see little for themselves in a united Germany. After all, there could be only one emperor. Self-interest led to their opposition to the actions at Frankfurt.

How much had German nationalism grown by 1850?

Frederick William IV again!

Despite his failure to support action in 1848–49, Frederick William was still keen on the idea of a united Germany – but only one of his own creation. He wanted to increase Prussia's role and influence within the German states. He proposed the creation of a federation of the German states within which Prussia would control the army and foreign policy. In effect, this would have created a *kleindeutsch* state. These proposals were put to delegates who had assembled at Erfürt. Not surprisingly, Austria reacted to the proposals with fury.

Faced with Austrian opposition, and fearing that the Prussian army was no match for that of Austria, the Prussians backed down. This was confirmed at a meeting of the two rivals at Olmütz in November 1850. Thus it was agreed that the *Bund* should be reconstituted as it had been prior to the events of 1848, i.e. dominated by Austria. This agreement signalled the complete triumph of Austria and the humiliation of Prussia. It appeared that the events of 1848 had already been forgotten and that the ideals of German nationalism were gone forever.

Source 7.5

Frederick William IV.

Activities

Teach a lesson

In groups of three or four, your aim is to teach a lesson to the rest of the class which is linked to the growth of nationalism in Germany by 1850. Your main resource for information is this textbook, but you must also find other sources of information to make you lesson lively and interesting.

- Negotiate with your teacher/tutor how long you have to prepare this lesson.

- Your lesson should be presented in an organised, mature and informative way.

- Planning is vital and every one in your group must participate. It would be helpful to assign tasks such as timekeeper, resource manager, encourager and recorder to note ideas and what was suggested.

continued ➡

Activities *continued*

- Your lesson should last no less than seven minutes and no more than ten.

- It must have visual material – PowerPoint is one possibility.

As in any lesson there are really important things for you to decide and aim for:

- What do you want your fellow students to be able to do and know at the end of the lesson? How will you share these expected outcomes with them?

- How will you assess the success of your lesson – in other words, what will you expect to see or hear your students doing to prove your lesson has been successful? How will you provide feedback to your students?

Sample Essay Questions

1 To what extent was failure of the 1848 revolution in the German states due to lack of leadership?

2 How important were the events of 1848–49 to the development of German nationalism?

Why was unification so difficult to achieve between 1815 and 1871?

By 1815 Europe had been at war for 23 years. Between 1792 and 1815 France had been the 'enemy' so in 1815 it was no surprise that the leaders of the European powers that had defeated France knew what they did not want to see develop in their countries – the forces of liberalism and nationalism that had been inspired by the French revolution. In addition, within the German states there were particular issues such as religion and the relationships between Austria and Prussia, which would hinder the development of nationalism in this period.

Germany after the Napoleonic Wars

There were many problems facing those who wanted to achieve a united Germany. The first, and perhaps the most serious, difficulty was to define exactly what was meant by 'Germany'. In the past, the Holy Roman Empire had occupied much of central Europe and many of the German states had been part of that. This had been destroyed by the French during the wars of 1792–1815. Napoleon had reorganised the old Holy Roman Empire into the Confederation of the Rhine. This, on the surface at least, resembled a more modern German state. However, the allies who met at Vienna in 1815 were determined to rid Europe of as much of Napoleon's legacy as possible and thus the Confederation of the Rhine was unacceptable.

Their solution was the German Confederation or *Bund*. In effect, this was a loose association of the 39 states that had emerged from the Vienna Congress. The actions of the *Bund* were to prove a bitter disappointment to German nationalists as, in the words of Ian Mitchell:

> ❝ *The Bund was more a means to perpetuate [continue] the division of Germany [than to unite it].*

Ian Mitchell, Bismarck and the Development of Germany, *1980*

Britain & Scotland and Germany

Source 8.1

Following the defeat of Napoleon I, representatives from Britain, Prussia, Russia and Austria met in Vienna to discuss the situation in Europe.

How did the structure of the *Bund* help to keep Germany divided?

The Bund was made up of representatives of the 39 German states who were nominated by their respective rulers. All decisions had to be unanimous. It is difficult enough for politicians to agree on anything, even with no opposition, so this was a difficult task. Also, the chairmanship of the *Bund* was given permanently to Austria. This was partly as a reward for being on the winning side in 1815. Austria was also considered to be the major German power; and was fiercely against the new ideas of nationalism and liberalism. Austria feared that these two forces would destroy its multi-racial empire and thus could be guaranteed to act as a repressive force throughout the *Bund*. The Austrian Emperor had set himself the task of consolidating a very strong Austrian Empire with the Danube River at the centre. At the same time, he did not want to see the creation of a strong northern rival in the shape of Prussia and thus he sought to keep the *Bund* weak.

The second problem was the issue of religion. The Thirty Years' War of the seventeenth century had been fought mostly within the German states. What emerged as a result was that the northern German states were mostly Protestant in religion, whilst the southern German states were mostly Catholic. The two major German-speaking states were Prussia (a Protestant state) and Austria (a Catholic state). Thus, small northern states

looked to Prussia for help and protection, whilst the small southern states looked to Austria.

The question of who should be included in any united Germany also created problems for the nationalists. There were two schools of thought:

Grossdeutschland: this group believed that any united Germany should include Austria, although there was no agreement on whether any part of her multi-racial empire should be included. Needless to say, Austria would never agree to joining a united Germany without her empire intact.

Kleindeutschland: supporters of this idea believed that a united Germany should not include any part of Austria and her empire.

As a result, defining what exactly was meant by 'Germany' was a real barrier to unification.

Another barrier to German unity came in the form of the leaders of the 39 German states. They were jealous of each other's power and position and did not wish to see their own power being lost to a rival so they wanted to maintain things as they were.

Source 8.2

The German Confederation after 1815.

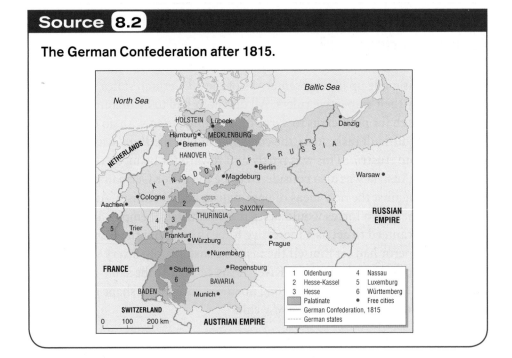

Another issue outwith Germany also contributed to the difficulties. None of the Great Powers of Europe wished to see the creation of a strong Germany which might upset the balance of power. Britain, Russia and Austria were all content to see the German states weak and divided.

Economic changes were also affecting the German states at this time. With Prussia's control of the Rhineland after 1815, the resources in that region were being used to develop Prussian industry. Austria suffered from a lack of natural resources such as coal and iron and lagged behind Prussia in industrial development. Austria was also excluded from the Prussian *Zollverein* and, as noted by the Austrian Chancellor of the time, Prince Metternich:

> ❝ *Little by little, under the direction of Prussia and because of common interests, the states which make up this union will compose a more or less compact body, acting in common.*
>
> Chancellor Metternich of Austria, 1818

Within the *Bund* there was a fear of Prussia. The smaller states resented Prussia's progress and were also fearful of being dominated by their large neighbour. Prussia had emerged in 1815 as a modern, efficient state with a highly effective army. The smaller German states therefore tended to side with Austria against Prussia in the *Bund*. Add to this the religious differences between Catholic and Protestant states and it is not difficult to see the challenges which German nationalists faced.

France was also a stumbling block to German unification. Since the days of the Revolution, France had wanted to expand its frontier with the German states to the natural barrier of the Rhine. This had been briefly achieved under Napoleon but the position was lost in 1815. Even worse, Prussia now occupied this area for the precise purpose of preventing French expansion and aggression into central Europe.

The leaders of France had no desire to see the creation of a strong country to her north-east. Under Emperor Napoleon III, France once again looked enviously towards lands occupied by the southern German states. Thus the opposition of France was an obstacle which German nationalists would have to get around.

Overall, it can be seen that those who wished to see a powerful, united Germany had many obstacles to overcome.

Activities

1 In this activity, make up at least ten questions which you would use to test someone's understanding of the main issues and developments in this period.

To construct good questions you must first understand the issues you are assessing and ensure your questions are not vague or ambiguous and that they focus on the key issues. One-word answer questions such as 'Who was…?' or 'When was…?' are not allowed.

Your questions should be mature, well presented and test real understanding. The purpose is to help learning, not to catch people out with really obscure or tricky questions.

When you have constructed ten questions, try them out on a partner. Can they answer your questions? And can you answer your partner's questions in turn?

The questions to remember are the ones to which you did not know the answer. They provide a guide to areas of knowledge where you are less confident.

9 Why was Germany united by 1871?

By the 1860s, there was a number of forces at work, some internal and some external, which would improve the chances of Germany achieving unity.

Within Germany, the idea of unity was gaining ground. In 1859, the German National Association was set up and by 1862 had in excess of 25,000 members. Prussia was also increasing in military, economic and financial strength – all vital ingredients if military action was being considered. The army appeared to be strong and the railway network had increased by more than 100 per cent since 1850. At the same time there was an increase in both coal and steel production. Prussia was also developing one of the best chemical industries in the world. Financially, the success of the *Zollverein* had provided the Prussian treasury with a large surplus.

Outside Germany, the success of the Italian nationalists encouraged nationalists throughout Europe. Meanwhile, Austria was weakened as a result of a number of factors. Firstly, its failure to support Russia in the Crimean War of 1854–56 against Britain and France had cost Austria the friendship of Russia. Tsar Alexander II never forgave Austria for this betrayal. Economically, Austria was suffering due to its exclusion from the *Zollverein* and within its multi-ethnic empire, minorities were demanding civil rights and, in some cases, independence from Austria. Amongst the leading powers of Europe there was also genuine sympathy for both the Italian and German struggles to achieve nationhood. Thus, Bismarck was operating in a much more favourable climate in the 1860s than his predecessors had faced in 1848–49. All he needed was an opportunity to show the Liberals that he was earnest in his claim to support their demands for unity, but on his terms. Prussia always came first, Germany second. He did not have to wait long.

Historian William Carr commented:

> " *The revolution in Germany [in 1848–49] had positive as well as negative aspects…Wider circles of the population began to take an interest in politics…Without the groundswell of public opinion favourable to unification which the revolution had created, the achievements of Bismarck would hardly have been possible.*
>
> *The revolution also helped clarify political attitudes and encouraged the formation of political associations, the forerunners of modern political parties.*

William Carr, A History of Germany, *1969*

Changes in Austria

Within Austria, events were underway to undermine its position not only within the *Bund*, but internationally as well. In 1852, the dominating political force of the Austrian Empire, Chancellor Schwarzenberg, died. Austria became entangled in events in south-east Europe, which meant it had to reach an agreement with Prussia.

Internationally, Austria had made a serious blunder. By failing to support its old ally Russia in the Crimean War against Britain and France, Austria lost an important friend. The Tsar, Alexander II, never forgave Austria for this betrayal. In 1849, with Austria's empire in revolt, the arrival of the Russian army had saved the day for Austria. During the Crimean War the Tsar expected that Austria would repay the favour. Failure to do so led to the destruction of an Austro–Russian friendship which would never be re-established. Russia would thus remain neutral in any future war concerning Austria – a neutrality that would inevitably favour Austria's opponents.

Commenting on the disruption of Austro–Russian relations, Feuchtwanger argues that Austria had lost all hope of support from Russia.

 The Holy Alliance [between Austria and Russia] was shattered for good and Austria had exchanged Russian support for hostility… Austria would astonish the world by its ingratitude towards Russia.

Edgar Feuchtwanger, Bismarck, 2002

Domestically, within the *Bund*, there was little that Austria could do to prevent the setting up of the *Nationalverein* (National Organisation) to struggle for the creation of a united Germany. This indicated that national feeling was an emerging force within the German states despite Austria's views, and within Prussia it led to the establishment of the Progressive or Liberal Party.

Source 9.1

Alexander II of Russia never forgave Austria for failing to support Russia during the Crimean War – something Austria would later regret.

Economic changes

Within Prussia, changes were also gathering pace. Under the direction of Manteuffel (1850–58), moderate reforms were being introduced, designed to increase the loyalty of the peasants towards the rulers of Prussia.

In the towns and cities, the government supported schemes to help factory workers. Again, the aim was to grant some of the workers' demands, thereby encouraging them to support the rulers of Prussia and turn away from revolutionary ideas.

> 66 *The Manteuffel regime was a bureaucratic regime, in general committed to the maintenance of the status quo, but tempered [balanced] by the perception that the maintenance of Junker privileges in all circumstances could not always ensure stability and social peace.*
>
> Edgar Feuchtwanger, Bismarck, 2002

Thus, in the 1850s, Prussia presented a paradox (a contradictory impression), alternating ultra-conservatism with carrying out progressive social reforms and encouraging the economic growth of the state.

In diplomatic and political terms, the tide was moving in favour of Prussia and, economically, Prussia was beginning to outstrip Austria. This would have far-reaching political, economic and military consequences for both powers.

The decade of the 1850s witnessed a growth and development of both the Prussian and German economies at the same time that Austria's was stagnating. These developments were due, in part, to the continued development of the *Zollverein* and the discovery of raw materials in the Rhine and Saarland, all of which were to be exploited by Prussia. On the other hand, Austria had few raw materials and was falling behind in an age where industrial strength was becoming increasingly important in politics.

Coal and lignite production (million tonnes)

Date	German Confederation	Austria	Britain
1850–54	9.2	1.2	50.2
1855–59	14.7	2.2	67.8
1860–64	20.8	3.6	86.3
1865–69	31.0	5.3	104.7

Why was Germany united by 1871?

Pig iron production (thousand tonnes)

Date	German Confederation	Austria	Britain
1850–54	245	173	2,716
1855–59	422	226	3,583
1860–64	613	216	4,219
1865–69	1,012	227	4,984

Length of railway line open (kilometres)

Date	German Confederation	Austria	Britain
1850	5,856	1,579	9,797
1855	7,826	2,145	11,744
1860	11,084	4,543	14,603
1865	13.900	5,858	18,439
1870	18,876	9,589	21,558

Why are these figures so important?

These tables show the widening gap between the output of the German Confederation and Austria. Figures for Britain have been added to allow for an international comparison.

In the 1850s, few people would have thought that Prussia would have unified Germany. Yet the figures clearly show that Prussia was moving ahead industrially at a rapid pace. The financial encouragement offered by the Manteuffel Government resulted in a rise in industrial production and foreign trade, as well as a rise in the standard of living. Although Prussia was no match for Austria politically, Prussia was economically the stronger country.

As Prussia grew stronger, the smaller German states realised the benefits of trade with Prussia. Working through the *Zollverein*, they benefited from the increased trade across the German Confederation. Austria was well aware of these developments and their implications. That is why she tried to develop an extended *Zollverein* to include Austria and those states still outwith the Prussian trade area. As Andrina Stiles commented, 'The intentions were political rather than economic.'

Source 9.2

The benefits of Custom Union.

Das Lichten eines Hochwaldes.

Prussia, too, was well aware of the motives of Austria and instructed its representative at the *Bund*, Bismarck, to oppose such moves. In this, Prussia was successful.

> *Bismarck fought every inch of the way to prevent Austria from making the Zollverein an integral part of the constitution of the Bund and thus gaining entry into it.*

Edgar Feuchtwanger, Bismarck, 2002

Bismarck arrives

The second half of the nineteenth century was the age of Bismarck. His skills, academic and diplomatic, were superior to all of his European contemporaries. He was to provide the dynamic leadership that had been so lacking during the events of 1848–49. There was hardly an event in Europe during this time that did not involve Bismarck, leading Ian Mitchell to comment that 'Bismarck was everywhere'.

Source 9.3

A young Otto von Bismarck.

Born into a Prussian *Junker* family in 1815, he at first gave some support to the ideas of liberalism and nationalism, but he later changed his mind. As he himself noted:

> " *My historical sympathies remained on the side of authority.*
>
> Otto von Bismarck, Reflections and Reminiscences, *1898*

His first real taste of the cut and thrust of politics came in 1851 when he was appointed as Prussian representative to the restored *Bund*. This was as a reward for his defence of the rights of the monarchy during the heady days of the 1848–49 Revolution. At first supportive of the ultra-conservative approach of the Austrians, Bismarck quickly grew frustrated by the Austrian tactics which he believed were designed to keep Prussia in an inferior position to that of its southern rival. In 1859, he was sent as ambassador to Saint Petersburg where he remained for three years. During that time, he realised it was essential for the security of Prussia to remain on friendly terms with Russia and he worked hard to maintain this all his working life.

In early 1862, he was sent to Paris as ambassador to the court of Napoleon III. Bismarck soon realised that French power was more apparent than real. He was contemptuous of Napoleon III, whom he regarded as his intellectual inferior and someone he could manipulate at will.

During a visit to the International Exhibition in London, he met one of Britain's leading Conservatives, Benjamin Disraeli, and is reported to have commented on his plans for the future.

> " *I [Bismarck] shall soon be compelled to undertake the conduct of the Prussian government. As soon as the army shall have been brought into such a condition as to inspire respect, I shall seize the first best pretext to declare war against Austria, dissolve the German Diet and give national unity to Germany under Prussian leadership.*
>
> Otto von Bismarck, 1862

There is doubt as to the authenticity of this statement. In hindsight it seems too good to be true! Nevertheless, the alleged conversation has been seized upon by some historians who argue that Bismarck always did have a long-term plan for the unification of Germany. Others, like A.J.P. Taylor, have argued that Bismarck followed a day-to-day policy, taking the course most likely to achieve his aims.

Meanwhile, in Prussia, King William wanted to improve his army but that would cost money. William's plans were blocked by the Prussian Progressive Party, which held a majority in the Prussian Diet (parliament).

When his plans were blocked by the Diet the King considered abdicating his throne. Such a move alarmed many of the King's ministers who feared that this would result in the triumph of the parliament over the King.

It was in this tense situation that von Roon, Minister of War, suggested to the King that Bismarck be recalled from Paris to help solve the dispute. Although reluctant to do so at first, the King eventually agreed and the now famous telegram, 'Periculum in mora, Dêpechez-vous!' (Delay is dangerous. Hurry!) brought Bismarck to Berlin to take up the challenge of becoming Prussian Chancellor.

Michael Gorman has argued that, at this stage, Bismarck had four aims:

- resolve the constitutional crisis
- raise Prussia above Austria in German affairs
- create a greater role for Prussia in European affairs
- maintain the position of the *Junker* class (the Prussian nobility).

His first task, though, was to solve the constitutional crisis – or he, too, might fall from power.

Bismarck's term in office saw the development of a new type of politics, referred to as *Realpolitik*. This was an emphasis on achieving realistic objectives rather than pursuing idealistic ambitions.

> **"** *Realpolitik meant that the age of ideology was ending and that politics would henceforth be dominated by material considerations and national interest rather than by abstract ideals.*
>
> Edgar Feuchtwanger, Bismarck, 2002

Such an outlook led Bismarck to conclude that, while striving to maintain the position of the monarchy, it had to be accepted that unification was likely to happen at some stage. His aim, therefore, was to control the process and to see established a German nation where the power and position of the Prussian monarchy would be maintained. He was willing to risk the disruption of Austro–Prussian relations in order to achieve this end. He feared being swept away on a nationalist tide and he saw the best form of defence as attack. He made this clear in his first speech to the Prussian Diet:

> *Germany does not look to Prussia's liberalism but to her power… Prussia must collect her forces and conserve them for an opportune moment which has already come and gone several times. Not by speeches and majorities will the great questions of the day be decided – that was the great mistake of 1848 and 1849 – but by iron and blood.*
>
> Otto von Bismarck, speech to the Prussian Diet, 30 September 1862

The Diet refused to give in to such bullying tactics. Bismarck therefore claimed that, since the constitution did not make provision for the resolution of a dispute between king and parliament, the final decision rested with the king who resumed the right to carry on the government without parliamentary approval. As the king retained control of the army, there was little parliament could do to challenge such an outcome.

However, Bismarck did realise that he could not continue to rule while he was permanently at war with the Diet. He sought some form of compromise by pursuing their foreign policy interests while denying them any control of domestic affairs. In this he had several advantages. The King dared not dismiss him lest his own position be again threatened. There is no doubt that the army reforms had been effective and the quality of the Prussian army had been improved. Economically, Prussia was thriving, due in part to the effects of the *Zollverein*. Finally, there had been a change in the relationships and roles of the Great Powers. Such conditions led Mosse to argue that Bismarck's success was not all of his own making:

> *Bismarck's task of unifying Germany was made easier by circumstances. If he played his hand with great skill, it was a good one in the first place.*
>
> Quoted in Cameron, Robertson and Henderson, The Growth of Nationalism: Germany and Italy 1815–1939, 1992

Bismarck's aims

Bismarck's long-term aim was to unite Germany under Prussian leadership in the hope of eliminating domestic parliamentary opposition. After all, these Progressives were also fervent nationalists and they could hardly object to policies that would bring about the very thing they wanted – a united Germany. Thus, it was to the area of foreign affairs that Bismarck turned. Here he was able to exploit several circumstances to his, and Prussia's, advantage.

The Kingdom of Poland had been swallowed up by Russia, Austria and Prussia at the end of the eighteenth century. The Poles were desperate to re-establish their independence and to that end there had been nationalist uprisings in 1830 and 1846, both ending in failure. In 1863, however, there was a large scale uprising in the Russian-occupied part of Poland. Fearing such a revolt might spread to Prussian Poland, Bismarck saw advantages in joint action with the Russians. He instructed Alvensleben, Prussian ambassador in Saint Petersburg, to reach an agreement with the Russians. The Alvensleben Convention allowed the Russian army to cross over the Prussian frontier in pursuit of Polish rebels. This agreement certainly assured Prussia of Russian gratitude. At the same time Bismarck was criticised by Britain and France, both powers being sympathetic to the ideals of the Polish rebels. Ironically, this criticism helped Bismarck and Prussia as it convinced the Tsar of the hostility of the western powers towards Russia and that Prussia was the only friend his country had in Europe. Again Bismarck rode roughshod over the opposition to the Convention in the Prussian Diet. So affairs elsewhere in Europe had allowed him to fulfil the liberal nationalist ambitions of the Prussian Progressives.

The Danish War

The Danish crisis was to be a clear illustration of the art of *Realpolitik* – the art of the possible, though not necessarily the desirable. Bismarck was not at all interested in the issues affecting the two duchies (territories) called Schleswig and Holstein, but he saw the opportunity that the crisis created for him to exploit it for his own ends. As Edgar Feuchtwanger wryly commented, 'Bismarck was above all a Prussian'.

Why was there a Danish crisis?

The Danish crisis arose over Schleswig and Holstein, two duchies on the border between Denmark and the German *Bund*, so called because they were under the supposed authority of a duke.

In 1863, the new Danish king, Christian IX decided to overturn the 1852 London Protocol, whereby Schleswig and Holstein were to be largely self-governing within the Danish kingdom. There was a large number of Danes living in North Schleswig, but the rest of the population of the two duchies of Schleswig and Holstein was mostly German in origin. Holstein was a member of the German *Bund*, but Schleswig was not. This complex situation explains the comment from the British Prime Minister, Lord Palmerston, that:

> 66 *Only three men have ever understood it [the Danish question]. One was Prince Albert [husband of Queen Victoria] who is dead. The second was a German professor who went mad. I am the third and I have forgotten all about it.*
>
> Lord Palmerston, May 1863

Bismarck realised that the German nationalists were outraged at the idea of the loss of Holstein as a member of the *Bund*. By taking action, he could portray himself and Prussia as a defender of German nationalism. Such an intervention would, coincidentally, prove to the Prussian Parliament that the army reforms they had so bitterly opposed had indeed been worthwhile. But Bismarck had to be careful. An earlier Danish attempt to annex (take over) Schleswig and Holstein in 1848 had resulted in Prussia acting alone and later being forced to back down by Austria. Bismarck did not want a repeat of that outcome so he had to convince Austria that it should join with Prussia in acting against the threat posed by the Danish demands. In addition, by taking the lead in defending the two duchies, Bismarck showed that Prussia was more interested in defending German interests than was Austria. This was why Bismarck formed an alliance with Austria in late 1863 to defend the position of the duchies within the Danish kingdom.

Another characteristic of Bismarck's policy can be identified in the war that would come. He always ensured that his enemy was isolated, with no hope of foreign assistance. This was achieved in 1864 as a result of a range of circumstances.

Britain was not in a position to help as it was first and foremost a naval power. Any help for the Danes would require the assistance of a major European land power and Britain wanted to avoid such entanglements. Additionally, Queen Victoria was sympathetic to the cause of German unity, especially so since the death of her husband, Prince Albert (himself a German), in 1861.

France was in no position to offer help as it was involved in a foreign adventure in Mexico during this time. Russia, too, was indifferent. As a result of the Alvensleben Convention, the Tsar considered Bismarck a friend.

Thus, the scene was set. Denmark, in clear breach of the London Protocol of 1852, found itself isolated, facing the combined forces of Prussia and Austria.

War with Denmark

The war began on 1 February 1864. Denmark was quickly overwhelmed by its enemies. In the resulting Treaty of Vienna the Danish king abandoned all claims to the duchies and, at the same time, joint rule (the term used to describe this is a condominium) over the two duchies was established by Prussia and Austria.

Source 9.4

Victorious Prussian troops march through the Brandenburg Gate at the end of the war against Denmark, 7 December 1864.

Debate over the role of Bismarck in this war continues.

> When the Schleswig-Holstein affair arose again, Bismarck intervened because he had to… It is clear that Bismarck wanted the question settled in the interests of Prussia.
>
> L.C.B. Seaman, Vienna to Versailles, 1964

> He [Bismarck] set the diplomatic challenge [to Austria] by skilful manipulation of a dispute between the Bund and Denmark. Prussia's intervention would indicate future leadership and raise Prussia's prestige.
>
> David Thomson, Europe since Napoleon, 1965

One of Bismarck's contemporaries, Friedrich Engels, pointed out that there was a difference in results and methods.

> In the matter of the Duchies, Bismarck had fulfilled the wishes of the bourgeoisie against their will. The fulfilment of national aspirations of the bourgeoisie was well under way, but the method chosen was not liberal.
>
> Friedrich Engels, quoted in Ian Mitchell, Bismarck and the Development of Germany, 1980

The Austro–Prussian War

The background to the conflict

Having dealt with the Danes, Bismarck now turned his attention to his great rival, Austria. He would have to expel Austria from the *Bund* if his aim of unification of Germany under Prussian leadership was to be achieved. Cameron, Henderson and Robertson are of the opinion that he planned for this:

> 66 *There is absolutely no doubt that he [Bismarck] set his sights on Austria once the crisis [Schleswig-Holstein] had passed over and worked to isolate her from the other European powers.*

Cameron, Robertson and Henderson, The Growth of Nationalism: Germany and Italy 1815–1939, *1992*

David Thomson would agree with this point of view, stating that 'There is no doubt that Bismarck wanted and planned for war against Austria.'

Source 9.5

Areas involved in the Austro-Prussian War 1866.

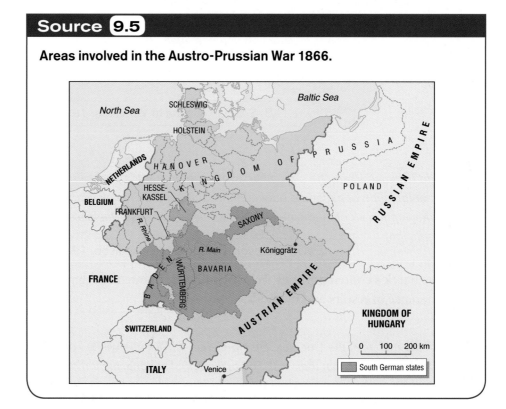

As before, Bismarck set about isolating his future enemy and destroying any support Austria might have among potential allies. However, war nearly came before he was ready.

After the end of the Danish War, joint rule had been established in the duchies. Whether Bismarck had intended this to fail is not clear. What is clear is that the two powers had very different ideas as to how the areas should be ruled. Bismarck was keen to annex the two territories, while Austria argued that their fate should be decided by the *Bund*. Belatedly, the Austrians realised that they had been drawn into a war from which they were to receive no real benefits. Talk of war between the two powers grew louder.

At this stage, Bismarck was not yet ready for war. His diplomatic and military preparations were incomplete and he had to play for time. In August 1865, by the Convention of Gastein, the two powers patched up their differences. The terms were that Prussia should rule Schleswig and Austria should rule Holstein.

Ian Mitchell has described this convention as a 'master-stroke' since it appeared that Austria had been outmanoeuvred by Bismarck: at any suitable time Bismark could pick a quarrel over the administration of the area, and to the smaller southern German states it appeared that Austria was only interested in acquiring more land for its empire. Crucially, Prussia now controlled Austrian access to its duchy, since Holstein was now surrounded by Prussian territory.

Now Bismarck could turn his attention to completing his war preparations. In a series of diplomatic moves, he isolated Austria prior to the outbreak of hostilities.

The isolation of Austria

France had to be persuaded to remain neutral in any such Austro–Prussian war. Bismarck played on the belief of Napoleon III that the German states should continue to be divided. He was also aware of the French emperor's desire to expand the territorial limits of France and, indeed, to undo the terms of the Vienna Settlement of 1815. Therefore, if Bismarck wanted to reshape the balance of power in Europe, he would need to offer the French something in return for their neutrality.

To this end, in October 1865, Bismarck 'happened' to meet Napoleon III at the resort of Biarritz.

Source 9.6

Bismarck and Napoleon III on the beach of Biarritz in 1865.

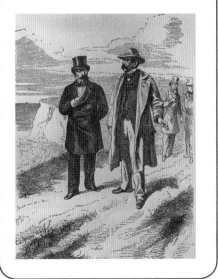

Why was Germany united by 1871?

No record of their meeting was kept and historians can speculate about what was agreed by retracing events from the war of 1866 and its aftermath. It would appear that Napoleon was convinced that if France were to remain neutral in any war between Prussia and Austria, France would be granted territorial compensation 'wherever French is spoken'. To Napoleon this certainly seemed to include Belgium and even parts of the west bank of the Rhine.

It was fairly safe to assume that Britain would not intervene. After all, it had not done so in 1864 and little had changed since then as far as Britain was concerned. Russia, too, could be counted on to remain neutral at the very least, as the Tsar was still grateful to Bismarck over Poland and had never forgiven Austria for failing to support Russia in the Crimean War of 1854–56.

Bismarck was also keen to have an ally in Europe, to prevent the image of a civil war between the two German powers attracting the interest of the other European nations. He settled on Italy for a variety of reasons. Firstly, the Italians regarded Austria as a stumbling block to the creation of a fully united Italy, since the Austrians still occupied the area of Venetia, the land around the city of Venice. Secondly, in any war involving Austria against Prussia and Italy, the Austrians would be at a military disadvantage of having to fight a war on two fronts.

Nonetheless, the Italians drove a hard bargain. Victor Emmanuel II of Italy did not really trust Bismarck and did not want to be left in the lurch if and when it suited Bismarck. So he insisted upon the following conditions for the proposed Prussian–Italian alliance:

- the alliance would last only three months
- Austria had to declare war
- Italy would declare war after Prussia had done so
- Italy would obtain Venetia as a reward.

The issue facing Bismarck became how to force conflict with Austria within the three month window of opportunity the Italian alliance had given him.

To this end, he began to increase pressure on Austria by declaring that elections to the *Bund* should be by universal male suffrage. This was totally unacceptable to all the other German states. However, before thinking that Bismarck had been transformed into a Liberal, it is necessary to note that once the offer was made, it was left to the other German states to respond. Their rejection of the proposal, a proposal welcomed by the Liberals, made them appear to be the reactionaries, while Bismarck could portray himself in a liberal light. This was just another example of his manipulation of political means for his own ends. After all, he had been at war with the

Liberals in Prussia over the issue of the army budget since coming to power. Here, he was again using events to try to score points and curry favour with the Liberals at home.

But Bismarck was also still faced with the need to force Austria to declare war if his Italian alliance was to hold. Fortunately, the actions of the Austrians helped Bismarck's cause. He was able to rouse Austrian anger over the issue of the latter's access to Holstein. Knowing that its army was inferior to that of its enemy, the Austrians had no option but to begin the mobilisation of its army ahead of Prussia. This was partly in response to Italian troop movements near Austria's southern frontier in late April 1866. Bismarck used this as an excuse to bully the Prussian king into mobilising Prussian forces. To the rest of Europe, the stationing of Austrian troops on Prussia's frontier gave the impression that Austria was the aggressor, and this meant Austria received no sympathy from them. In fact, Austria was so isolated in Europe that when the other European powers proposed a conference to avert war, the Austrians refused to attend. Bismarck, despite the upset that it might cause to his Italian alliance, had accepted. Thus, it seemed to Europe that it was Austria which was responsible for the war.

War with Austria

Austria decided to take the initiative, ended talks over Schleswig and Holstein and instead proposed that the matter should be decided by the *Bund*. This was against the terms of the Gastein Convention and Bismarck ordered the Prussian army to invade Holstein on 10 June 1866. On the same day, Bismarck raised the tension even more by proposing the creation of a new German state, excluding Austria, and calling for elections to a national assembly to create it. This was the final straw and on 14 June 1866 Austria declared war on Prussia. All of Bismarck's carefully laid plans could now come into effect. Bismarck also issued ultimatums to Saxony, Hanover, Bavaria, Württemberg and Baden to join with Prussia or be considered enemies. They all sided with Austria, as expected, and with their rejection of Bismarck's demands, the Austro–Prussian War began.

With the outbreak of war, Bismarck was careful to keep German nationalists 'on side'. Part of the declaration of war on Austria included a call to all Germans:

> 66 *Let the German people come forward in confidence to meet Prussia. Let it help to promote and make secure the peaceful development of our common Fatherland.*

Prussian Declaration of War, 1866

Why was Germany united by 1871?

Thus, Bismarck was able to portray Prussia as fighting to establish a modern unified German state.

Source 9.7

The Battle of Königgrätz, 3 July 1866.

The states of Hesse and Saxony (allies of Austria) were immediately invaded by Prussia once war began and neither offered any resistance. By the end of June, the resistance in the other German states had collapsed. In the south, the Italians were badly mauled by the Austrians but this was largely irrelevant to the course of the war. They achieved no more and no less than Bismarck had expected, keeping 200,000 Austrian troops involved in that area. This greatly helped the Prussians at the only major battle of the war, the Battle of Königgrätz (or Sadowa) on 3 July 1866.

The war was a stunning success for Prussia. It had been assumed that the two sides were evenly matched but Prussian superiority over Austria bore fruit. Using its extensive rail network, the Prussians were able to move large forces relatively quickly to the battlefront. The telegraph was used to enable Prussian generals to communicate directly back to Berlin. Despite superior Austrian artillery, the Prussian army was better organised, had better rifles and used superior tactics in combat. After sustaining large casualties the Austrians accepted overwhelming defeat.

Bismarck wanted to end the war quickly and was prepared to offer the Austrians generous terms. He argued that, 'We have to avoid wounding Austria too severely'. Bismarck had achieved his aim of pushing the Austrians out of German affairs. He also feared a severe Italian defeat and there was always the possibility of French intervention. An armistice was signed at Nikolsburg on 26 July 1866 and the war was formally concluded by the Treaty of Prague of 23 August 1866.

The terms of the treaty were beneficial to Prussia but were also accepted by Austria as generous:

- Austria gave up the territory around Venice called Venetia which was transferred to the Italian kingdom.
- Austria was expelled from the *Bund* but would lose no land and only had to pay a small amount of compensation.
- Schleswig, Holstein, Hesse–Cassel, Frankfurt and Hanover were all taken over by Prussia.
- The 21 states north of the River Main were to form a North German Confederation under Prussian leadership.
- The southern German states were to remain independent, but were forced to pay large indemnities to Prussia.
- The southern German states were also forced into military alliances with Prussia.

The results of the war were spectacular. Despite Austria's defeat, she was soon able to re-establish good relations with Prussia. French power and prestige had been reduced. At home, Bismarck was now regarded as a national hero. Even the Liberals forgave him for his unconstitutional rule of Prussia from 1862 and passed an Indemnity Act giving retrospective approval for his actions, as well as giving him a reward of £60,000.

Feuchtwanger has viewed this as a major departure in Bismarck's career.

> 66 *It was the turning point when Bismarck ceased to be a gambler living precariously and became the towering, overwhelming figure that dominated Germany and Europe for the next twenty five years.*
>
> (Edgar Feuchtwanger, Bismarck, 2002)

The Franco–Prussian War

Although acclaimed by many German nationalists as a hero, Bismarck was well aware that their aims had not yet been fully satisfied. The states north of the River Main were now united in the North German Confederation, but the position of the South German states still had to be settled. One solution would have been for Prussia simply to have annexed these to the Confederation. However, this would have exacerbated the suspicion between the north and south over the issue of religion and Prussian domination and the result would have been nothing but hatred towards Prussia. Bismarck slowly came round to the idea that the southern German opposition could only be overcome by creating an enemy who was even more dangerous to the South German states than Prussia.

> **"** *I did not doubt that a Franco-Prussian war must take place before the construction of a united Germany could be realized.*
>
> Otto von Bismarck, Reflections and Reminiscences, *1898*

The background to war

There were several issues creating tension between France and Prussia, the first being Napoleon III's belief that he should be rewarded for remaining neutral in the Austro–Prussian War. Bismarck rejected Napoleon's demands but asked for them to be put in writing 'for future consideration', which the French emperor was happy to do. These demands were then promptly leaked to the press, causing fury amongst the South German states as much of the compensation was to be taken from their lands. Thus, reluctantly, the South German states were drawn into Prussia's orbit through the need for a powerful 'big brother' to oppose the French bully. This fear of French expansionism had played into Bismarck's hands.

Bismarck also seemed to encourage, or manoeuvre, Napoleon III in his ambitions to increase his influence, once over Luxembourg and once concerning Belgium. On both those issues Bismarck must have known the rest of Europe, and especially Britain, would be unhappy about French actions. On both occasions Napoleon III had to climb down. Certainly, relations between France and Prussia were chilly by the end of the 1860s.

What was the Spanish Candidature?

Bismarck still required an excuse for war, a way of isolating France and a means of entrapment of the South German states through military alliances, economic ties and bribery. Such an opportunity arose in Spain.

The Spanish 'Candidature' is a classic example of how Bismarck used a situation, not of his own creation, to advance his own aims. As McKichan wrote, 'in 1870, Bismarck was clearly using the question of the Spanish throne to stir up trouble with France'.

> **"** *It seems certain that Bismarck engineered the dispute [between France and Prussia] by supporting the Hohenzollern candidate for the Spanish crown. Bismarck wanted war. He believed the time was ripe.*
>
> David Thomson, Europe since Napoleon, *1965*

The Spanish Parliament was seeking to appoint a new king following the removal of Queen Isabella. Bismarck saw a further chance to antagonise France by placing a Prussian prince on the throne of Spain, thereby encircling France. He knew that France would never accept such a proposal, since it threatened its security. The Prussian king, William I, was also reluctant, fearing it might lead to war with France. Bismarck bullied him into nominating a minor member of the Hohenzollern royal family, Prince Leopold, as Prussia's nominee.

Bismarck had hoped to have the deal signed before the French found out about his scheme. However, France did find out and was enraged. The French ambassador to Prussia, Benedetti, was instructed to demand the withdrawal of Leopold, or Prussia would face war.

King William had always been against the candidature and he pressured Leopold into withdrawing. When news of this reached Bismarck, he was appalled at the king's actions and even thought of resignation.

Napoleon III now saw the chance to exact revenge on Prussia in general, and Bismarck in particular, for all of the previous humiliations. Benedetti was again instructed to demand that the Hohenzollern candidature would never be renewed. Breaking diplomatic protocol, he approached the Prussian king on the street in the town of Bad Ems. William told Benedetti that he could not make such a guarantee about future actions. He then sent a telegram to his chancellor, detailing French demands and a summary of what had taken place.

Source 9.8

The Ems Telegram from 1870 about the meeting between William I of Prussia and the French ambassador Benedetti. Edited by Bismarck, it resulted in the French declaration of war against Germany.

Bismarck saw the potential for action. Editing what became known as 'the Ems Telegram', he altered its tone, making the meeting at Ems seem like a snub to the French. The edited text was released to the press.

The French politicians were incensed at this version of events. They demanded that the emperor declare war on Prussia, an action to which he reluctantly agreed on 19 July 1870. This allowed Bismarck, once more, to pose as the innocent victim of French aggression.

Historians have clear views on Bismarck's actions. Seaman believes that:

> *The action of Bismarck [editing and releasing the Ems telegram] was his own free choice and he must bear responsibility… Bismarck could have done little had not his victims made themselves his accomplices [helpers] by their folly [foolishness].*
>
> L.C.B. Seaman, Vienna to Versailles, *1964*

Feuchtwanger summed up the situation neatly when he wrote:

> *A war with France breaking out under the right circumstances might well be the catalyst for bringing the South German states to the side of Prussia.*
>
> Edgar Feuchtwanger, Bismarck, *2002*

Bismarck had ensured French isolation by publishing French demands for compensation in the South German states. Alarmed by the possible French threat, the military alliances with the South German states came into effect and all decided that they would have to back Prussia in a war of national defence against France.

The outcome of the Franco–Prussian War

Once again, Prussian military and economic strength was decisive. The French army was defeated at Worth in August 1870 and again, at Sedan, in the following month. The fleeing army was besieged in Metz, and Paris was surrounded and fell in January 1871. The emperor, Napoleon III, was captured and a republic was declared. Finally, on 18 January 1871, in the Hall of Mirrors in the Palace of Versailles, William I, King of Prussia, was proclaimed German Emperor.

The peace treaty which followed the war was very different to the one with Austria. The Treaty of Frankfurt, signed in May 1871, was harsh. Cameron, Henderson and Robertson are of the view that the Treaty of Frankfurt was a cruel, victor's peace. The treaty annexed (took away) land from the French. For example, Metz and Strasbourg were annexed to Germany and France had to pay an indemnity (compensation) of £200 million within four years. But it was the fate of Alsace–Lorraine that was to create a festering sore in French–German relations, until 1914 provided the opportunity for French revenge. L.C.B. Seaman commented that, 'A France deprived of Alsace–

Lorraine by war guaranteed the insecurity of Germany', while D.G. Williamson added, 'In retrospect few would disagree that this [annexation of Alsace–Lorraine] was a miscalculation of great consequence.'

Source 9.9

1 September 1870 – Napoleon III and Bismarck on the morning after the Battle of Sedan. France was left bitter and wanting revenge against Germany.

Source 9.10

Founding of the German Empire on 18 January 1871. King William I of Prussia is proclaimed German Emperor in the Hall of Mirrors at The Palace of Versailles.

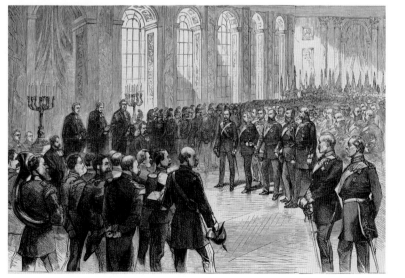

How important was Bismarck to German unification?

There are differing views on the overall importance of Bismarck to unification.

Until the mid-twentieth century, it was generally accepted that Bismarck alone was responsible for the unification of Germany under Prussian domination. Otto Pflanze wrote that:

Only under the stimulation provided by Bismarck for his own political ends did German nationalism begin to move the masses.

Quoted in Cameron Robertson and Henderson, The Growth of Nationalism: Germany and Italy 1815–1939, *1992*

This view was perpetuated, even by Hitler, who commented that 'It was he [Bismarck] who created conditions which rendered possible the creation of Great Germany.'

However, since that time, the interaction of other factors has been considered. Williamson argues that 'Bismarck did not fashion German unity alone. He exploited powerful forces which already existed – economic, liberalism and nationalism.' Mosse contends that 'Bismarck's task of unifying Germany was made easier by circumstances', while Medlicott notes that 'His [Bismarck's] admirers often exaggerate the extent of the obstacles in his path.' Aronson believes that Bismarck was an opportunist and Stiles thinks 'his policies can best be described as flexible'.

Other later writers have taken a stance more hostile to Bismarck. The German historian Eric Eyck argues that 'German unification in the third quarter of the nineteenth century was a natural and desirable development', while others would emphasise the economic dominance of Prussia as a natural lead to political unification – what Seaman would refer to as 'coal and iron' rather than 'iron and blood'.

Activities

1   Re-read this chapter carefully.

2   Make two lists, the first showing the **actions of Bismarck** which led to unification and the second listing **the actions of others**.

3   Use the evidence from the lists to reach a conclusion about the role played by each in the unification of Germany. Present your views about which of these was more important and provide relevant evidence to support your opinion.

Sample Essay Questions

1   How important was Bismarck to German unification?

2   To what extent was the unification of Germany due to the Prussian army?

The Empire created by Bismarck in 1871 was destroyed as a result of defeat in the First World War. Debate continues to rage over whether Emperor Wilhelm II and his advisers deliberately opted for war as a way of removing the pressures for change which had built up within Germany by 1914. What is certain is that the Germany which emerged from war was very different from the Kaiser's Germany of 1914. In November 1918 Germany collapsed politically. Revolution broke out across Germany. The Kaiser abdicated. Germany was defeated and leaderless. In this chaos the new German Republic was born.

Source 10.1

Events in Germany, 1918–1920

October 1918
General Staff insisted upon democratisation of the German government. Prince Max von Baden became Chancellor, responsible to the *Reichstag*.

Late October/Early November
Surrender of Germany's allies. Mutiny began in the German navy at Kiel.

9 November
Abdication of the Kaiser was announced.
Ebert, leader of the Social Democrat Party (SPD), became Chancellor.

11 November
Armistice came into effect

January 1919
Attempted coup by extreme Left wing – the Sparticist Uprising. This was crushed by the army and the *Freikorps*.
SPD won the largest number of seats in the *Reichstag*, but fell short of an overall majority. Coalition government formed.

28 June
Treaty of Versailles signed. Bitter opposition to the terms of this treaty within Germany.

January 1920
Attempted right wing coup – the Kapp *Putsch*. The Army was sympathetic to the coup. It was suppressed by the calling of a general strike amongst German workers.

As the timeline in Source 10.1 indicates, the new country had to face severe challenges to its very existence in its formative years. Simpson believes that:

> " *The Weimar Republic was born out of the external defeat of the German Empire and the internal collapse of its system of government. It is an open question whether the Weimar Republic could ever have overcome the disadvantages which attended its birth.*
>
> *William Simpson*, Hitler and Nazi Germany, *1991*

The Weimar Republic – Born at a bad time!

Right from the start the Republic had to overcome the hostility of large sections of the population and the media. Finlay McKichan has put forward the theory that this was 'a Republic nobody wanted'. He supports this by arguing that:

- democratic reforms were only introduced in October 1918 in a cynical attempt to get better terms from the Allies
- the revolution of November 1918 was not extensive enough
- there were divisions among those who claimed to be the supporters of the regime.

What evidence is there to support this view?

It is argued that military defeat was not accompanied by political change. During the war, the German Empire had effectively been run by Generals Hindenburg and Ludendorff. Following the Allied victories in August 1918, it was these leaders who argued for a 'revolution from above'. The German generals knew that political change was inevitable and they wanted to control it. This led to the appointment of Prince Max von Baden, with the cynical view that such a liberal civilian government would achieve better terms with the allies at any future peace conference. This 'revolution from above' resulted in a number of changes to the way Germany was run.

The army came under the control of the civilian government. For the first time, ministers were responsible to the *Reichstag* and the formerly undemocratic voting system in Prussia was reformed to give 'one man, one vote'. The negative side of such positive developments was that the new leaders of Germany were the ones who had to carry the burden of Germany's defeat and not the emperor and his generals, who were regarded as national heroes in the eyes of many people. The blame for defeat was placed firmly onto the leaders of the new Republic.

Revolution from below!

However, there were developments elsewhere that threatened the new Republic. As in Russia, workers' and soldiers' soviets had appeared. These groups, or councils, demanded a much more thorough change in the way Germany was ruled. They led mutinies in the German navy and law and order appeared to be under threat. Such developments frightened many within Germany and this forced the new government to make an alliance with the army in order to restore order. Such an alliance was to have long-lasting implications for the new regime.

Another reason put forward for the collapse of Weimar democracy by 1933 was that its supporters were also divided. John Hiden noted that:

 Although the time seemed ripe for a remodelling of society and a clean break with the imperial past, German socialists were neither fully prepared for revolution nor united.

John Hiden, The Weimar Republic, *1974*

The socialists under Ebert, who now led the government, had been brought up in the tradition of working towards an improvement in working and living conditions by reaching agreements with the ruling elite. They did not provide the dynamic leadership which could exploit the new situation. Indeed, the socialists themselves were split. The extreme left wing of the party had already split from the majority, forming the Independent Socialists or USPD, which had opposed the war and refused to co-operate with the emperor's government. They refused to co-operate with Ebert.

Thus, the opportunities presented by the abdication of the emperor could

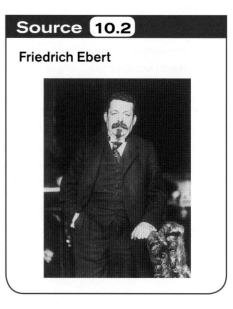

Source 10.2

Friedrich Ebert

not be fully exploited to the benefit of the new regime. Evidence to support this 'missed opportunity' idea included:

● the secret agreements made between the leaders of the new government and the Army. The Army only agreed to help Ebert when it became clear that the new leadership would not pursue any revolutionary ideas and that there would be respect for law and order.

● the agreement reached between the employers and the major industrial firms. This resulted in the German revolution taking a quite different path from that of Russia. Instead of workers overthrowing employers, in Germany, they continued to co-operate in order to preserve the peace. Such a tactic had the added benefit of avoiding any marked deterioration in workers' living standards by maintaining full employment. This accommodation was bitterly opposed by the workers' and soldiers' councils.

What was Ebert to do? In justification of his policy, he argued that,

> " We had to make sure that the Reich machine did not break down; that it was able to maintain our food supplies and the economy. We needed the experienced co-operation of experts. We would have faced failure in a few days.
>
> Friedrich Ebert, 1921

Historians, too, have tried to defend the actions of Ebert. In his book, *Weimar and the Rise of Hitler* (1968), A.J. Nicholls has argued that

> " Ebert and his Social Democrat colleagues were eager to re-establish order in Germany and to organise the election of a National Assembly. They had no reason to believe that the sort of Germany they wanted could not be created without the aid of existing officials.
>
> Quoted in Finlay McKichan, Germany 1815–1939, 1992

Finlay McKichan adds:

> " The Social Democrats seemed less concerned to keep on good terms with the Independent Socialists who were members of the same government.
>
> Finlay McKichan, Germany 1815–1939, 1992

McKichan implies that the creation of stable government was more important than any idea of working class solidarity.

Why did the Nazis achieve power in 1933?

Meanwhile, several main issues threatened the security of the new Republic:

- pressure from the left and right wing political parties
- the impact of the Treaty of Versailles
- the Constitution and economic instability.

In January 1919, the leaders of the USPD, Karl Liebknecht and Rosa Luxemburg, supported an armed uprising, known to history as the 'Spartacist Rebellion'.

It was at this point that the alliance of the new government and the old imperial army came into operation. Ebert feared for the existence of his government and he urged the army to suppress the uprising. Employing returning ex-soldiers in groups known as *Freikorps*, the state used all means at its disposal to suppress the uprising. No mercy was shown, with Liebknecht and Luxemburg being murdered before they could stand trial. This action destroyed any hope of co-operation between the different wings of the socialist groups. The USPD refused ever again to work with the majority socialists, even when faced by the dangers posed by Hitler and his party. It was also during this time that the government temporarily moved out of Berlin for its own safety. It moved to the relatively quiet town of Weimar – hence the name, the Weimar Republic.

The Treaty of Versailles

Another big problem for the new government was that it had to deal with the consequences of the Treaty of Versailles. Here was a classic example of the old regime escaping the responsibility for the defeat of Germany in 1918.

It was up to the new rulers of Germany to accept the terms of the treaty, or risk the renewal of war. Thus the German delegates who stood before the Allied leaders in June 1919 were powerless to change the Treaty. At the same time a myth developed about Germany being 'stabbed in the back'. This claimed that the German army had been undefeated in 1918 (like all myths, it did contain an element of truth, as German soldiers still occupied areas of north-east France in November 1918), and that it was the discontents at home, the democrats, the Jews, the Communists and the Socialists, that had forced Germany into the armistice of November 1918, with all its consequences. The reality was that the German army was about to collapse, and the democratisation of Germany in October 1918 was a ploy on the part of Hindenburg and Ludendorff to squeeze better peace terms from Germany's enemies.

However, there is little doubt that the stigma of the 'November criminals' (the German politicians who signed the Treaty) hung like a giant shadow over the period of Weimar Germany.

The Treaty was hated by most Germans. There were two main areas of complaint.

The first was loss of territory. Although France regained Alsace and Lorraine, most Germans probably expected to lose these areas as Germany had taken them from France at the end of the 1870–71 war. The people spoke French and their restoration to France had been a main aim of French foreign policy from that date.

Source 10.3

Writing the Treaty of Versailles in the Hall of Mirrors at the Palace of Versailles

In addition, the Saar coalfields were to be transferred to France for fifteen years as compensation for the German destruction of French coalfields as they retreated in 1918. The final decision as to who would control the area would be made following a plebiscite (a referendum), to be held in 1935.

On the other hand, land lost to Belgium (Eupen and Malmedy), Denmark (North Schleswig) and to Poland (Posen, West Prussia and the upper part of Silesia) angered many Germans. They believed that these changes were contrary to the Allies' own principles, especially US President Wilson's desire to see the frontiers of the 'new Europe' to be drawn along 'recognisable lines of nationality'. Wilson had also claimed that one of the causes of the war was the existence of many minority peoples living within countries which were alien to them. It was difficult to reconcile these ideas with the Treaty arrangements that left millions of German-speaking people

Why did the Nazis achieve power in 1933?

in the so called 'Polish Corridor' and given that East Prussia was now separated from the rest of the country.

Additionally, some three million German-speaking settlers now lived under the government of Czechoslovakia. A union between Austria and Germany (*Anschluss*) had been forbidden by the terms of both the treaties of Versailles and St Germain. Internationally, all of Germany's colonies were taken from its control and effectively given to Germany's former enemies. There was thus a sense of grievance and injustice over these terms, leading to discontent with the Weimar rulers.

The second cause of complaint was the way the Treaty was agreed. In May 1919, the German delegates were handed a draft with one month to agree to its acceptance or face the renewal of war. Faced with this threat, the German delegation had no option but to sign the treaty on 28 June 1919. However, the German government and people were never reconciled to the idea of reparations or German 'war-guilt'.

Hugo Preuss bemoaned the terms of the treaty for Germany:

> " If the empire was born out of the brilliance of victory, the German Republic was born out of its terrible defeat...The criminal madness of the imposed Versailles settlement was a shameless blow...the Reich constitution of Weimar was born with a curse upon it.
>
> Quoted in Peter Merkel, The Origin of the West German Republic, *1963*

Many would agree that the lasting damage caused by the Treaty was one of the major reasons for Nazi success by 1933. The disarmament of Germany was another blow to the once proud German military tradition. After the losses of the war, the Allies were determined to prevent another conflict. The German army was reduced to no larger than an internal police force (100,000) and the navy was drastically reduced in size, including no submarines and no air force.

The Allied claim that Germany had caused the war was also bitterly resented. Article 231 forced Germany to accept responsibility for the war. To German eyes, these terms created the impression that the treaty was designed to humiliate Germany. The treaty was to cast a long shadow over the history of the Weimar Republic, leading historians like A.J. Nicholls to claim that 'The German public was in no way prepared for a harsh peace', and that the treaty led many to support groups such as the Nazis during the 1920s.

Hugo Preuss noted that:

> " *Many Germans blamed the Allies for the weakness of democratic Germany. The lament of so many...decent Germans about the burdens...inflicted by the Allies upon an innocent Germany... undermined democracy and facilitated [made easier] the rise of Hitler.*
>
> *Quoted in Peter Merkel,* The Origin of the West German Republic, *1963*

Getting rid of the treaty became the central part of the programme of Nationalist and Nazi propaganda.

A more balanced analysis from John Hiden suggests:

> " *The Versailles treaty certainly did not doom the Republic from birth, but it did create particularly troublesome dimensions to existing internal conflicts and contradictions which had, to some extent, survived the revolution.*
>
> *John Hinden,* The Weimar Republic, *1974*

The long-term damage of the treaty is summed up by A.J. Nicholls arguing that, 'The real damage the treaty did was to disillusion more moderate men who might otherwise have supported their new Republic.'

Thus, although not now regarded as a main reason for Nazi success, there can be little doubt that the Treaty of Versailles was fully exploited by the Nazis for their own ends. Hitler's uncompromising stance against the Treaty of Versailles and the Weimar Republic as well as his oratorical skills placed him in a strong position when, after October 1929, the German people sought out a strong leader for Germany.

The problems of German democracy

Another area where historians have tried to explain the collapse of democracy in Germany centres around its new constitution.The Weimar Constitution has been called 'the world's most perfect democracy – on paper'.

For the first time, all Germans, male and female, could vote if over the age of twenty. The *Reichstag* was to be elected directly by the German people whilst the Upper House, the *Reichsrat*, contained representatives of all the German states. Elections were to be determined by a form of proportional representation. This meant that a party obtaining fifteen per cent of the total votes cast would receive fifteen per cent of the seats in the *Reichstag*.

The President, the head of state, was to be elected directly by the people. He had extensive powers which included:

- being head of the armed forces
- appointing the Reich Chancellor
- having the right to dissolve the *Reichstag* and call fresh elections
- under Article 48, he could suspend the constitution and rule directly by decree in times of crisis.

The difficulties that this constitution produced were, firstly, that proportional representation led to the growth of many small parties.

The number of parties, combined with the proportional representation voting system, made it impossible for any one party to gain a majority in the *Reichstag*. Coalition governments of two or more parties were thus necessary. However, as each party had its own ideas about how Germany should be run, these coalitions often fell apart. This led to frequent elections and the appearance of a weak form of government.

The table below shows the major political parties during the 1920s:

DNVP	German National People's Party
NSDAP	National Socialist German Workers' Party
DVP	German People's Party
Zentrum	Centre Party
DDP	German Democratic Party
SPD	German Socialist Party
USPD	United German Socialist Party
KPD	German Communist Party

Secondly, as head of state, the President could suspend the constitution and rule by himself in times of emergency. On the one hand, it has been argued that this conditioned the German people to the idea of rule by one man. On the other hand, its use after the collapse of the German economy in October 1929, and the inability of parties to agree terms for a coalition, did help to keep some form of government going during this difficult period.

Although the government had been happy to use the army and the *Freikorps* to suppress the left-wing uprising of 1919, by the start of 1920 the *Freikorps* in particular were beginning to pose a threat to law and order. In early 1920, the government wanted to disband elements of these units. This led to a march by some *Freikorps* members in Berlin. In terror, the government fled and a new government was declared under Wolfgang Kapp. Ebert, the chancellor, asked the army for help. When this aid was not forthcoming, the government called a general strike. Berlin was paralysed

as public transport workers, workers in the power industries and even civil servants heeded the call to strike. The result was that Kapp and his *Freikorps* followers withdrew from Berlin.

Evidence of the dependence of the new democratic regime on the power structures of Imperial Germany came to light in the aftermath of this Kapp *Putsch*. Whereas the leaders of the Sparticist uprising had been murdered without trial, the leaders of the 1920 coup were let off fairly lightly.

The lasting impact of this was to destroy any loyalty between the people and government after its flight from Berlin.

Economic problems

It is now generally agreed that the idea of reparations was not very well thought through. It was to prove impossible for Germany to meet its treaty obligations of £100 million per year for 66 years. This would have resulted in Germany's final payment for the First World War being made in 1986. The cost of financing its own war effort and the loss of land and resources under the Treaty of Versailles severely weakened the German economy.

The background to the hyper-inflation of 1923 had little to do with economics. In 1922, the German government signed a Treaty of Friendship and Co-operation with the other outcast nation of post-war Europe – Russia. Amongst the secret provisions were clauses allowing German troops to train on Russian territory, thereby getting round some of the military restrictions of the Treaty of Versailles. Thus, the French, in particular, were looking for an excuse to put Germany back in its place.

Early in 1923, the Germans had defaulted on payment of telegraph poles and some tons of coal. Seizing on this, the French and Belgian governments acted jointly to occupy Germany's richest industrial area, the Ruhr. The German Government called on the workers of the Ruhr to meet such aggression with passive resistance. In effect, this meant a strike in most industries in the Ruhr. This area was the heart of the German economy. As it slowed, and then almost stopped, the effects were soon felt across Germany. Unemployment rocketed and inflation began to run away, as can be seen in the table below:

Value of US dollar to German Mark	
January 1922	$1 = 80 Marks
January 1923	$1 = 18,000 Marks
November 1923	$1 = 4,420 million Marks

This resulted in the German economy spiralling out of control. People were often paid twice a day; barter replaced cash exchanges, and many middle class families lost everything that they had saved over generations.

However, the German Government can be blamed partly for the impact of hyper-inflation. It certainly suited them since it could repay debts at a fraction of their real value.

The Government authorised the printing and over-printing of German banknotes without the gold reserves to support it. Those in circulation lost all face value. People in employment were just able to survive, but those on fixed incomes, like pensioners, were ruined. It was this sense of hopelessness and unfairness that led many people to yearn for 'the good old days' of strong rule under the emperor. Although the causes of hyper-inflation are extremely complicated, to the ordinary German it was the

Source 10.4

Children playing with German banknotes during the period of hyper-inflation.

fault of a government that had accepted reparations payments as part of the Treaty of Versailles. It also seemed that the Government was not doing much to prevent the crisis of 1923 from deepening. Many, especially amongst the middle class, never forgave the Weimar Republic for the humiliation that was forced upon them in order to survive. It was this group that was to prove most receptive to the seductive message of Nazism. The economic events of 1923 also had political consequences, one of which was an attempt by an extreme right-wing group to seize power in Bavaria.

Hoping to capitalise on the misery of 1923, in November Adolf Hitler tried to seize power in Munich. He intended to force the Government to give way to a new, right-wing force. However, the event was a fiasco and Hitler was captured, put on trial for treason and sentenced to five years in prison. He was released after less than one year, but the Nazis had been brought to national attention. Hitler's contempt for Weimar democracy can be seen in this conversation held while prisoner in Landsberg Castle:

> ❝ *When I begin active work, it will be necessary to pursue a new policy. Instead of working to achieve power by an armed coup, we shall have to hold our noses and enter the Reichstag.... If outvoting them takes longer than outshooting them, at least the results will be guaranteed by their own Constitution.*
>
> Adolf Hitler, 1924

Source 10.5

Hitler during his imprisonment at fortress Landsberg, February to November 1924.

With the suppression of the Beer Hall Putsch (coup) and the arrival of US loans as part of the Dawes Plan, the situation in Weimar Germany began to improve. However, the memory of the 'economic whirlwind' of 1923 was to remain long in the memories of the German people. For Hitler, too, a change of tactics was necessary. Respect for law and order was ingrained in the German people. His failure at the Beer Hall Putsch convinced Hitler that the Nazis would have to achieve power by legitimate political means. He also set himself the task of improving the efficiency of the party, developing the effectiveness of its organisation (particularly the propaganda machine) and reasserting his personal control. Such was his success that Simpson has concluded that, 'By the end of 1926 Hitler's position [within the party] was unchallenged.'

The Rise of the Nazis

To understand how the Nazi Party was able to achieve success in Germany, it is necessary to look at the origins of the Party and what it stood for, and how Hitler transformed it into an effective political force within Germany.

The beginnings of the Party are to be found in the depression that followed Germany's defeat at the end of the First World War. Many small political groups emerged at this time and Hitler, now acting as a political instructor for the German army, was sent to investigate an obscure group by the name of the German Workers' Party. Despite its name it was not a socialist or communist group, but instead was violently nationalistic (*völkisch* in German) in its outlook. Such ideas appealed to Hitler and he was invited to join the Party. Such were his speaking skills that he soon came to dominate meetings. He was able to influence the creation of new and more popular policies for the Party and persuaded the members to change the name to the National Socialist German Workers Party (*Nationalsozialistiche Deutsche Arbeiter Partei*), or NSDAP for short, in 1920.

It should be remembered that the Nazi Party was but one of many so-called *völkisch* parties in Germany at this time. They shared common features such as being right wing, nationalist in outlook, anti-Weimar Government and bitterly opposed to the Treaty of Versailles. They also shared a common racist outlook in that keeping the German race pure was essential to maintain the strength of the nation (*Volk*). The main differences with the Nazis were Hitler's abilities as a public speaker and his conviction that his policies would save Germany.

Nazi Ideology

Till his suicide in 1945, Hitler never deviated from the ideas he had set out in *Mein Kampf*. Its main themes were:

- *Nationalism* – the Nazis called for all Germans to be united under one leader. Thus, Germans living in Austria, Czechoslovakia and Poland should be reunited in one Greater Germany. This point also emphasised that the Treaty of Versailles and the Treaty of St Germain should be destroyed.

- *Anti Semitism* – the Party was violently anti-Jewish in its outlook. The Jews were blamed for strangling the German economy and being responsible for the 1923 hyper-inflation. They also were accused of 'stabbing the German army in the back' in 1918, and of being pro-Communist in outlook. Such a group had no place in a pure *völkische* regime.

However, such ideas had little appeal in Germany after 1924 as a result of the success of Gustav Stresemann.

A Golden Era?

The time between 1924 and 1929 is often called the 'Golden Era of the Weimar Republic' and coincided with the coming to power of Gustav Stresemann, German Foreign Minister from 1924 till his death in 1929. Among his achievements, he was able to persuade the French to leave the Ruhr, having promised that Germany would restart payment of reparations. This helped pave the way for the introduction of the new currency in 1924, the *Rentenmark*, which formed part of the Dawes Plan for the economic recovery of Germany. This plan also reduced the burden of German reparation repayments and was backed by massive foreign loans designed to get German industry back to work. By 1927 the German economy had recovered to levels not seen since before the First World War. The recovery compared favourably with the conditions in both Britain and France in the 1920s.

In foreign policy, Stresemann was able to end Germany's diplomatic isolation from the rest of Europe. He improved relations with France, agreeing to the Locarno Pact of 1925 which guaranteed the Franco–German border established by the Treaty of Versailles. His speeches claiming that Germany now only wanted to pursue a peaceful foreign policy were rewarded when Germany was allowed to enter the League of Nations. This showed that Germany was seen as an equal, no longer an outcast, and recognised its status as a great power.

Source 10.6

German Foreign Minister Gustav Stresemann addressing the League of Nations after Germany was allowed to join in 1926.

Was democracy in Germany secure by the end of the 1920s?

During the Stresemann years the appeal of the Nazis vanished. The government was meeting the needs of many of its citizens and gaining support among many political parties. These years were 'lean ones' for the Nazi Party as:

 Stresemann and his times denied the Nazi fire the oxygen of misery and it was all but extinguished.

> *Cameron, Robertson and Henderson*, The Growth of Nationalism: Germany and Italy 1815–1931, *1992*

On the other hand, the Republic still faced serious problems. Parliamentary democracy was still in its early stages. There was division over social, economic, political and religious grounds amongst the supporters of the Republic. The army was, at best, lukewarm to the Government and this indifference was common also among the civil service. Finally, the economic structure was unbalanced due to an over-reliance on foreign loans which left the Republic subject to the fluctuations of the international economy.

It will never be known whether the Weimar Republic could have gone on to win the loyalty of the German people or reverse the terms of the Treaty of Versailles and so remove the shame of 1919, because it was not given the time. In 1929, the Wall Street Crash had disastrous consequences for the German economy and the Weimar Republic. As McKichan states, 'In 1929 it faced a disastrous economic blizzard in which much of what it had achieved was blown away.'

The collapse of democracy

The causes of Germany's economic problems after 1929 were to be found on the other side of the Atlantic. With the collapse of the New York Stock Exchange in October 1929, the US demanded the repayment of its loans to Germany. This set off a chain reaction in Germany which soon saw the return of mass unemployment and fears of a return to the hyper-inflation days of 1923.

Unable to agree on how to deal with the problems, the socialist-led coalition resigned in March 1930 and the last democratically elected government of Germany till 1991 left office. Finlay McKichan has argued that, 'Hitler would have remained on the fringe of politics had it not been for the Great Depression which began in 1929, and the hardship it brought'.

Source 10.7

Events in Germany, 1929–1933

October 1929
Wall Street Crash. US demands repayment of German loans. German unemployment rises.

March 1930
Brüning of the Centre Party becomes Chancellor. Government tried to balance budget. Cuts in pay of civil servants and unemployment benefits. Brüning only able to run Germany by use of presidential decree – Article 48 of the Constitution.

September 1930
Reichstag elections. Nazis increase number of seats from 12 to 107. Communists also increase number of seats from 54 to 77. Fall in support for the SPD from 153 to 143 seats.

1930–32
Unemployment rises to 6 million

April 1932
Presidential elections held. Hitler comes second to Hindenburg.

July 1932
Brüning is replaced as Chancellor by von Papen. New elections held. Nazi representation increases to 230. KPD numbers increase to 89. Fall in support for SPD to 133. No viable government can be formed.

November 1932
New *Reichstag* elections. Nazi seats fall to 196. KPD seats fall to 81. SPD seats fall to 121.

December 1932
von Papen is replaced as Chancellor by General von Schleicher. Political intrigue between von Papen and Hitler.

30 January 1933
Hitler appointed Chancellor – head of a coalition government.

27 February 1933
Reichstag burns down in middle of election campaign. Hindenburg signs decree for the 'protection of the people and the state'.

5 March 1933
Nazis win 288 seats – only 43.9 per cent of votes cast. Although banned, 12.3 per cent of electorate voted for KPD. SPD won 120 seats. Therefore, the Nazis never won a majority in a free election.

Why did the Nazis achieve power in 1933?

To ensure the government continued to operate, President Hindenburg used the powers granted to him under Article 48 of the Weimar constitution. This set a dangerous precedent that the Nazis would later exploit to set up their one-party state. A new government, led by the Centre Party leader, Brüning, was now asked to tackle the economic crisis. Brüning cut Government spending but the economy continued its downward spiral. The following chart shows the increase in unemployment in Germany in a year on year basis.

Source 10.8

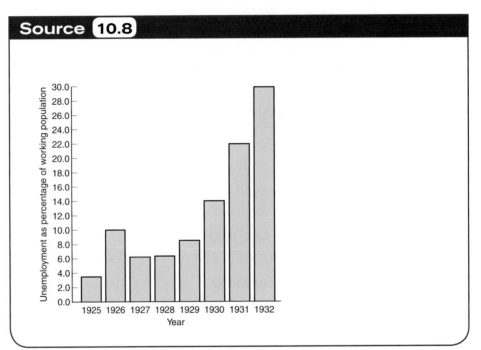

Source 10.9

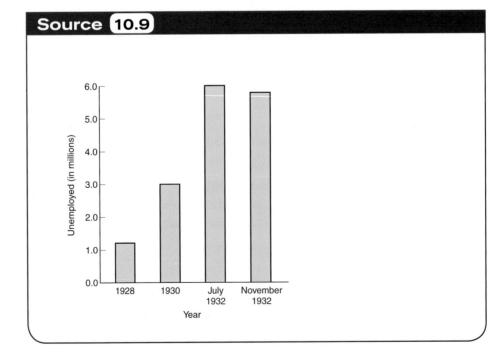

It is all too easy to see a direct correlation between the increasing rate of unemployment and the growth in support for both the Nazis and the communists, but recent research has shown that not all of the unemployed voted for the Nazis. Catholics remained loyal to the Centre Party and unemployed working men continued to support the socialists and communists. Rather, it appears that fear of unemployment, rather than unemployment itself, tended to make many people look to the Nazis as a way out of the crisis. The Nazis gained most votes from farming and small-town, lower middle classes.

> 66 *The Party derived enormous benefit from its continued effort to win over the rural population during the crisis. To vote for Hitler was for many a rejection of the existing system.*

> John Hiden, The Weimar Republic, 1974

There is no doubt that Germany suffered much more than either Britain or France during this period and that Hitler exploited this misery to the full.

Mary Fulbrook noted that:

> 66 *Its [the Nazis] growing electoral support in the elections of 1930 and 1932 was directly related to the growth of mass unemployment and the growth of political instability in this period.*

> Mary Fulbrook, Hitler, 2004

Why did the Nazis gain power?

L.E. Jones has argued in *German Liberalism and the Dissolution of the Weimar Party System* (1988) that the Nazis managed to win support from a wide cross-section of society in this time of crisis.

However, there is much more to the eventual Nazi success than just the economic situation, though this is considered to be the crucial factor. Many theories have been put forward in order to explain why Hitler was able to achieve power by January 1933.

Firstly, there was the appeal of the Nazi Party. They offered something to everyone, even if their policies were contradictory. Farmers were promised fair prices for their produce but consumers were lured by the prospect of cheap prices for food. The workers were promised jobs and a fairer share of the national wealth – the *socialist* part of National Socialism. At the same time, businessmen were promised the destruction of Communism and a

curb on the power of workers. The army was promised the destruction of the Treaty of Versailles and a programme of rearmament.

The middle class was offered the destruction of the Jewish banks and many were attracted by the Nazi promise to create a society based on merit, not birth or wealth.

The young, unemployed of Germany were offered hope in place of despair. As these forces came together in the summer/autumn of 1932, the Nazis were propelled towards power.

Another factor worthy of note is the effective use of propaganda. David Welch in *The Third Reich – Politics and Propaganda* (2004) argues that people who voted for the Nazis did so not so much because of their conversion by propaganda, but because doing so would lead to a material improvement in their lives. But McKichan believes that the role of Goebbels, in charge of Nazi propaganda, was vital in helping to spread the Nazi message.

Source 10.10

German Propaganda Minister Joseph Goebbels

The Nazis exploited the new media of radio and cinema to get across their message, in addition to the more traditional ones of political posters, marches, rallies and the newspapers. Hitler's alliance with Hugenberg, the newspaper and cinema owner, allowed the Nazis to reach a mass audience, as this was the era when people went to the cinema about twice a week. Indeed, the authors of *The Growth of Nationalism* argue that 'The Nazis were among the first to realise the persuasive power of this medium [cinema].'

Another aspect of Nazi success was their efficiency in election campaigns. The four general election campaigns, in addition to two rounds of presidential voting in 1932, and the referendum on the Young Plan in 1929, had given the Nazis plenty of time to perfect their electoral techniques. Rothnie has suggested that, 'Never has any Party prepared for power more thoroughly than the Nazis during the period 1925–1933.' To this end, they used their greatest electoral asset, the public speaking abilities of Hitler himself. This has led the authors of *The Growth of Nationalism* to conclude that, 'He was the Nazi Party's greatest electoral asset.'

The SA (Brown Shirts) was also used to great effect during the Nazi rise to power. As well as acting to protect Nazi rallies and meetings, they also created the sense of instability and violence which the Nazis promised to end!

How far were the Weimar politicians responsible for the collapse of democracy?

Sadly, the Weimar Republic and its politicians cannot escape responsibility for the success of Hitler and historians have long debated to what extent the political weaknesses of the Weimar Republic contributed to Nazi success. John Hiden argues that, 'Brüning took up the Chancellorship during a period of profound public disillusionment with the parliamentary system.'

Some of the weaknesses were long standing – as old as the Republic itself.

The inability of the SPD and the KPD to co-operate in the face of the threat posed by their opponents can be traced back to the suppression of the Spartacist Uprising in 1919. Both parties had socialist beliefs but rather than unite to face a common enemy, they continued to squabble over the nature of Socialism most appropriate for Germany. Indeed, the resignation of the SPD-led coalition in March of 1930 over the proposed cuts in unemployment benefit led to the rule of Brüning, the so-called 'Hunger Chancellor', and its associated difficulties.

The political intrigue between President Hindenburg, von Papen and General von Schleicher also damaged democracy in Germany. They were more interested in setting up an authoritarian government that would restore law and order than in maintaining democracy.

Brüning fell from power when he lost the confidence of the president, but when Franz von Papen succeeded Brüning he was unable to put together any real support in the *Reichstag*. At the next election the Nazis gained the largest single block of votes in the *Reichstag*, but even so Hitler rejected the offer of the vice-chancellorship. Behind the scenes, the fate of von Papen was sealed by the actions of General von Schleicher who replaced von Papen in December 1932. Unhappy at his dismissal, von Papen entered into an alliance with Hitler to oust von Schleicher. Fatefully, von Papen agreed to Hitler's demands to be made Chancellor, with von Papen as his Vice-Chancellor. Never was a man proved so utterly wrong than von Papen when he announced on the eve of Hitler's appointment as Chancellor on 30 January 1933, 'We've hired Herr Hitler.'

Why did the Nazis achieve power in 1933?

Activities

Your task is to create a walk-through gallery explaining why the Nazis came to power in 1933.

You will need:

- A sheet of A3 paper or flip chart paper
- Felt tip pens
- Your notes on this chapter

The class will be divided into groups of five.

Each group takes one of the following topics and writes it in the centre of the A3 sheet:

- Weaknesses of the Weimar Republic
- Resentment towards the Treaty of Versailles
- Economic difficulties
- The appeal of the Nazis
- Weaknesses and mistakes of opponents

Each group has to write a reason linked to the heading using the coloured pen provided.

The groups then move on to the next sheet, taking their pen with them, and add their views to those already written, trying not to look at what is already there.

The process continues till all groups have noted something on every sheet.

The sheets are then displayed and the pupils walk through the gallery to show the collective responses of the class.

Pupils can then summarise the class findings as part of their revision of this part of the course.

Sample Essay Questions

1 How important were the political weaknesses of the Weimar Republic in the Nazis' rise to power?

2 To what extent can Nazi success be explained by the effect of the economic depression from 1929 onwards?

11

How did the Nazis maintain power in Germany between 1933 and 1939?

11

Hitler's aim was now to establish a country that reflected Nazi beliefs and ideology. This process was to be known as *Gleichschaltung*, or co-ordination. By 1939 the Nazis had extended their control to every corner of German life. It is necessary to evaluate the methods used by the Nazis in order to assess how effective and successful they were.

Source 11.1

Events in Germany, 1933–1934

Timetable of '*Die Machtergreifung*' (Seizure of Power)

30 January 1933

Hitler appointed Chancellor. New *Reichstag* elections called.

27 February 1933

Reichstag burned down. Hitler announced a communist plot. Construction begun of concentration camp at Dachau to 'hold enemies of the state'.

March 1933

Decree for the Protection of the People and the State passed.

5 March 1933

Elections held. Nazis gained 288 seats – only 43.9 per cent of the vote.

23 March 1933

With support from the DNVP, the Enabling Act (Law for Removing the Distress of the People and the Reich) was passed. KPD deputies (81) had been arrested; 26 SPD Members were 'missing'. The Nazis achieved the two thirds majority needed. The Government could now issue laws without the President's signature.

2 May 1933

All Trade Unions banned. Nazi Labour Front set up.

July 1933

Nazis reached agreement with the Roman Catholic Church – priests not to take part in politics. All political parties except Nazis banned.

January 1934

State governments abolished. *Gauleiters* were appointed by Hitler.

30 June 1934

'Night of the Long Knives' – all opposition to Hitler within the Party was eliminated.

August 1934

Hindenburg died. Hitler became President as well as Chancellor and took the title – *Führer* – 'Leader'.

Hitler was the head of a coalition government but he had nothing but contempt for Weimar democracy. Hitler's first task was to persuade President Hindenburg to call an election to see if the people of Germany agreed with his appointment as chancellor. Hitler was to exploit this to meet his own ends.

On 27 February 1933, one week prior to the election, the *Reichstag* burned down under mysterious circumstances. Hitler claimed it was the signal for the beginning of a communist seizure of power and persuaded the president to sign the Decree for the Protection of the People and the State. This removed all guarantees of civil liberties from ordinary Germans and was to remain in force till 1945. To ensure his success, Hitler had already appointed Herman Göring who controlled the police force across two-thirds of Germany and wielded immense power. To bolster state police forces, the SA and the SS (Schutzstaffel or 'protective squadron', a separate Nazi paramilitary force) were to be given the status of an auxiliary police force. Despite this, the results of the election were not what Hitler had hoped. Although polling 43.9 per cent of the popular vote, Hitler still did not have the majority needed to change the constitution. As Hildebrand noted, 'The [Nazi] Party was never returned to power by a majority of the German people.'

Quite simply, Hitler had his communist opponents arrested and on the day the vote was taken on The Law for Removing the Distress of the People and the Reich (referred to as The Enabling Act), 26 members of the SPD were 'missing'. Thus, Hitler now had the necessary two thirds majority he needed. The effect of this act was that democracy in Germany was effectively over as emergency decrees could now be issued even without presidential authorisation, a step towards a one-party totalitarian state.

Finlay McKichan noted:

> " *The Nazis used the powers given to them by the Enabling Act to dispose of any organisation which might oppose or obstruct them and to ensure that people in positions of authority supported them*
>
> *Finlay McKichan, Germany 1815–1939, 1992*

Hitler now had to secure the exclusive authority of the Nazi Party within Germany and remove all forces opposed to him. His first actions were against opposing political parties and organisations. Trade unions were banned on 2 May 1933. The Reich Labour Front was set up to 'protect the interests of the workers'. However, all strikes were declared illegal and the Labour Front, under Robert Ley, was given power to fix wages. Opponents within the trade union movement were quickly arrested and sent to the newly established concentration camp at Dachau, close to Munich. Others saw the danger and kept quiet. On 22 June, the SPD was banned. Most of the other political parties broke up, the last being the Catholic Centre Party which disbanded on 5 July 1933. On 14 July, a new law was passed declaring the Nazi Party the sole legal political party. Thus, a combination of 'persuasion' and the use of the law saw the removal of German civil rights.

The professions were the next target for the Nazis. Anti-Nazi members of the civil service were dismissed and Jewish officials were forced to resign their posts. Thus, many previously unemployed now gained work, reducing unemployment and allowing the Nazis to claim they had solved Germany's economic crisis. However, the Nazis did require an efficient civil service to enable government business to be conducted. On 7 April 1933, the Law for the Re-establishment of the Professional Civil Service was announced. This law allowed for the dismissal of Nazi opponents but since in the eyes of most Germans the Nazis had come to power legally, there was no justification for obstructing their policies and the civil servants went about their daily business.

By 1936, 32 per cent of teachers and an even higher percentage of doctors, 45 per cent, were members of the Nazi Party. What is not so clear is if these groups believed in Nazi ideology or saw membership as a way of furthering their careers. What is clear is that there would be little or no opposition to Nazi rule from these quarters.

Within the legal system, anti-Nazi judges were removed and replaced by those sympathetic to the regime. A People's Court was set up in 1934, led by reliable Nazi judges. This was followed in 1935 by the passing of the law against 'Acts Hostile to the National Community'. This all-embracing law allowed the Nazis to persecute their opponents in an apparently legal way. In this way, the rule of law in Germany was slowly undermined and the rights of German citizens were severely restricted. However, as David Welch wrote, 'Without being necessarily staunch Nazis, many judges and lawyers welcomed the Nazi regime in 1933 for their promise to restore a more authoritarian notion of 'law and order'.' Thus German citizens had lost their right to an independent judicial system.

Organised religion could have acted as a focus for opposition to the Nazis. At first the Nazis were worried about a possible conflict with the Catholic and Protestant Churches in Germany so they tried to reach agreements with them. In July 1933, the Nazis reached an agreement (concordat) with the Catholic Church. Under Hitler's *Concordat*, the Catholic Church was guaranteed religious freedom and the right to run its own affairs without state interference. In return, the Church pledged not to interfere in politics.

The Protestant faith, representing 45 million Germans, was organised into 28 different churches. On 4 April 1933, Ludwig Müller was appointed as National Bishop to lead all German Protestants in a German Christian Church. This new church was as equally dominated by Nazi beliefs as by religious teachings. Despite all attempts, the voices of opponents would not be stilled. Ministers such as Martin Niemöller and Dietrich Bonhöffer showed great courage in speaking out against the regime. Nonetheless, by 1937, the Protestant churches had lost their ability to defend themselves against the state.

How did the Nazis maintain power in Germany between 1933 and 1939?

A major issue facing Hitler was the position of the army and the role of the president. Hindenburg was an old man and might not live much longer. In order to declare himself *Führer*, Hitler would require the support of the army. However, Ernst Röhm, the leader of the SA, was demanding that there be a second revolution in which the army and the SA would be merged. The latter now comprised 2.5 million men, well-practised in street fighting and the use of violence to achieve their ends. They now represented a threat to many within Germany whom Hitler could not afford to offend. Hitler needed to calm these fears and began to consider the elimination of Röhm and the SA as a solution to his difficulty.

On 30 June 1934, the leaders of the SA were murdered, arrested or disposed of, as were other opponents to Hitler within the Nazi Party. The real winner from this 'Night of the Long Knives' was Heinrich Himmler, whose SS had carried out the murders. There followed a major shift within Germany towards a police state under Himmler's direction. This reached its peak in 1939 with the creation of the RSHA (*Reichsicherheithauptamtes* – a central organisation controlling all the means of Nazi persecution) under Reinhardt Heydrich.

The full meaning of the Nazi chant, '*Ein Volk, ein Reich, ein Führer*' now became perfectly clear to all. Hitler was the German state and any opposition would be ruthlessly destroyed.

Following the death of Hindenburg on 2 August 1934, the army kept its part of the agreement. Hitler proclaimed himself *Führer*. In a plebiscite on 19 August 1934, 89.93 per cent agreed with Hitler's action and he was now in a more secure position. As Simpson concluded:

 In a rapid series of moves, Hitler consolidated his own position, extended the authority of the Reich government over the individual German states and crushed all potential sources of opposition.

Simpson, Hitler and Nazi Germany, *1991*

Creating a Nazi society – 'The carrot'

Before he came to power, Hitler promised to create a *Volksgemeinschaft*, a 'national community' of interests. He now had to put this into practice. Once again, the tactics involved persuasion, threats and fear of the Nazi state.

The youth of Nazi Germany was the key to setting up a 'thousand year Reich'. Thus it became a prime target of the Nazi machine. Its youth policy was aimed at turning boys into soldiers and girls into submissive housewives and mothers. At first membership was voluntary but it became compulsory in March 1939. National organisations were set up for different

age and gender groups. For boys at the age of ten, membership of the German Young People (*Deutsches Jungvolk*) was available. On reaching the age of fourteen, they could graduate to the Hitler Youth (*Hitler Jugend*) where activities such as camping and shooting were designed to prepare the male youth of Germany for the next conflict. So successful was this move to 'regiment' the youth of Germany that by 1936, some 60% of all young Germans belonged to some Nazi organisation.

For girls, the attitude of the Nazi regime was, at best, ultra-conservative or, at worst, sexist. At the age of ten, girls could join the League of Young Girls (*Jungmadelbund*), moving on to the League of German Maidens (*Bund Deutscher Madel*) at the age of fourteen. In both organisations, emphasis was placed on the three Ks – *Kinder, Kirche, Kuche* (Children, Church, Kitchen) which taught girls to accept their role as a mother and a wife in the new regime. At the age of 17, girls could join the *Faith and Beauty* organisation, specialising in home economics and preparations for marriage.

It was crucial for the Nazi Party to win the support of young people if its aims were to be fulfilled and the effectiveness of the state in indoctrinating the youth of Germany is an issue of great debate. The traditional view is that most young people were willing participants in the Nazi youth organisations and were enthusiastic in their support of the state. However, this view has been challenged as other evidence suggests that the regime was only partly successful in its integration of young people.

Overall, there can be little doubt that some young people were totally won over by the state. Opposition from groups such as Edelweiss Pirates was more like teenage rebellion to authority than opposition to specific Nazi ideology. Youth organisations and activities were some of the more subtle methods used to capture the minds of the German young and to indoctrinate them in Nazi methods and ideology. The other, more direct method was by Nazi control of education.

Source 11.2

By 1936, 60 per cent of all young Germans belonged to a Nazi organisation, like these boys in the Hitler Youth.

Education was viewed as vital to secure the acceptance and continuation of the Reich. To begin, the teaching profession had to be purged of any potential opposition to Nazi ideas. Jewish teachers were immediately dismissed from their posts. Teachers were encouraged to join the National Socialist Teachers' Alliance whose task was to indoctrinate teachers in Nazi beliefs. Many teachers were won over to Nazi ideology and wanted to share this with their young classes. Specialist schools were set up. These included the Nazi military academies, or 'Napolas', where the emphasis was on military training. On leaving, pupils were expected to join the *Waffen* SS. The next generation of Nazi leaders was to be trained at the '*Ordensburgen*' where the curriculum featured much political training.

The Nazis also altered the school curriculum to reflect their point of view. Sport was encouraged to raise physical fitness. There was a strong emphasis on the teaching of history to show students the glory of the German past. Biology was corrupted to explain Nazi racial theories of German superiority. *Rassenkunde* (racial studies) was a new subject introduced to show the supposed superiority of the Aryan race. It is fair to say that during this period there was a fall in academic standards and teachers lost much of their professional status. They were now regarded as a tool of the state, rather than an independent profession.

Nazi economic policy

The Nazis had come to power just as the world economic crisis was easing. By the end of 1932, German unemployment was beginning to fall but the Nazis took the credit for this general upturn in the world economy. The dismissal of enemies of the state and many Jewish workers created jobs for unemployed Germans. However, by themselves, these measures would not have been enough. It is necessary to look at Nazi economic policy to see if they did achieve an economic miracle, as Göbbels often claimed.

The Nazis began a massive programme of public works that employed tens of thousands of Germans. These included public building works (*Arbeitsdienst*) as well as the creation of the motorway network. As men were taken on under these schemes, the economy would benefit as, firstly, they were now employed and not claiming benefits from the state, so government expenditure would fall. At the same time, they now entered the labour market and began to pay tax, increasing government revenue. With money to spend, they created demand in other areas of the economy for goods and services, thereby encouraging employment in these sectors.

Another factor contributing to Germany's economic recovery was the programme of rearmament, secret at first but openly flouted from 1936 onwards with Herman Göring's policy of 'guns before butter'. Overall, the

Nazi Government had distorted the economy in order to prepare for war. In the short term, it certainly created jobs, but by 1939 there were severe pressures building up in the German economy.

However, evidence suggests that most German workers found that there had been a slight decline in their overall standard of living. In an attempt to deflect criticism from the regime caused by this decline in living standards, the Nazis set up organisations like *Kraft durch Freude* (KdF, or Strength through Joy). This organisation offered subsidised holidays and activities. The regime even tried to produce a people's car or *Volkswagen*, which would be mass produced at reasonable prices. Although the first model appeared in 1938, increasing demands for military vehicles meant that it was never fully developed under the Third Reich. Another attempt to persuade the workers that the Nazi state was delivering for them was the *Schönheit der Arbeit* (Joy at Work), the aim of which was to persuade employers to improve working conditions by, for example, providing better ventilation, improved lighting and providing workers with nutritional meals.

Yet despite all these measures, the Nazi regime remained suspicious of the working class. Unrest amongst workers led to strikes in Berlin in 1936 and increasing mistrust towards the Government. It proved impossible for the Nazis to end working-class loyalty to the socialist and communist parties.

Source 11.3

Construction of the Reich's Autobahn, 1933.

To gain power, Hitler had appealed to the *Mittelstand* (lower middle class) of German society. He had promised a society based on merit, not birth or wealth. Despite these early promises, the Nazis never really delivered on them as they found they depended on the traditional classes to prop up the Hitler regime and provide leaders for the armed forces. The need to re-arm Germany also led to dependence on big business and thus Nazi promises to these groups remained unfulfilled.

The farmers of Germany had delivered a solid bloc of votes for the Nazis between 1929 and 1933. Although regarded as the true representatives of the *völkisch* community, there were limits to what the Nazis could do for this sector. The farmers had been badly affected by the collapse of world trade in 1929 and were faced with crippling interest repayments to banks. Hitler did attempt to help this group by raising taxes on food entering from abroad and by cancelling debts run up by farmers. Despite this aid, the regime needed to feed a growing population that was slowly gearing up for war. Despite state subsidies and financial inducements to stay on the land, the Nazis were unable to stop the drift away from the countryside as more and more left in search of a better living.

Nazi family policy was dominated by the Women's Front (*Frauenfront*), set up in May of 1933. Women were encouraged to have more children with financial inducements, tax reductions and family allowances for low income families. There was even an attempt to integrate women into the structure of the *Volksgemeinschaft* with the setting up of organisations like the National Socialist Womanhood and German Women's Enterprise.

Mary Fulbrook noted:

 The experiences of women varied dramatically... Here as in so many areas of the Third Reich, rhetoric and reality were often self-contradictory. Hitler's views on women, which now appear extraordinarily sexist, were at the time fairly representative.

Mary Fulbrook, Hitler, *2004*

Nazism and Anti-Semitism

For most people, the Nazi regime is linked forever to the persecution of the Jews and, uncomfortable as it may be, the anti-Semitism of the Nazi state was a factor in its popularity with many Germans. In power, the violently anti-Semitic Nazi Party sought first to isolate, then discriminate against and destroy the Jews living within Germany's borders.

 Anti-Semitism was not only the core of Nazi ideology, but the Jewish stereotype that developed from it provided the focal point for the feeling of aggression inherent in the ideology.

David Welch, The Third Reich – Politics and Propaganda, *2004*

The first steps were taken in April 1933 with the organisation of a nationwide boycott of Jewish businesses. Other actions soon followed. On 7 April 1933, Jews were dismissed from their posts within the civil service. This was the beginning of a whole range of moves against the Jewish professions. Doctors, lawyers, teachers and dentists, among others, were prohibited from working. In October 1933, Jews were forbidden from working in journalism.

In September 1935, the Nuremburg Laws stripped Jews of their German citizenship as well as outlawing sexual relations or marriage between Germans and Jews.

Source 11.4

Smashed windows of a Jewish shop in Berlin in the aftermath of Kristallnacht, November 1938.

In 1938, using the excuse of the murder of a German diplomat in Paris by a Jew, the regime authorised the so-called *Kristallnacht*. Shops and homes belonging to Jews were attacked, as were many synagogues. After this the Nazis introduced new laws excluding Jews from participation in the economic life of Germany and Jewish pupils were expelled from schools. Many Jews now sought refuge abroad, away from a regime that so obviously threatened their very existence.

It would be wrong to argue that these policies of the regime illustrate some long term plan to deal with the 'Jewish question'. Also, no evidence exists to support the idea that all Germans in 1933 were in favour of

Source 11.5

Prisoners working as part of a construction team in Dachau concentration camp, 1938.

How did the Nazis maintain power in Germany between 1933 and 1939?

any extremist or violently anti-Semitic policy. In *A Social History of the Third Reich*, Richard Grunberger argued that *Kristallnacht* divided Germany into three distinct sections of opinion, 'The shocked but silent at one end, the looters and vicarious sadists at the other – and a broad middle stratum of inert bystanders'. Nonetheless, the effect of this policy was summed up in the following poem:

> 66 First they came for the communists, and I did not speak out – because I was not a communist;
> Then they came for the socialists, and I did not speak out – because I was not a socialist;
> Then they came for the trade unionists, and I did not speak out – because I was not a trade unionist;
> Then they came for the Jews, and I did not speak out – because I was not a Jew;
> Then they came for me – and there was no one left to speak out for me.

> Poem attributed to Pastor Niemöller – a bitter opponent of the Nazi regime

Nazi Propaganda

There has been much debate about the effectiveness of Nazi propaganda in maintaining the regime in power. Great emphasis has been placed upon the role of Joseph Göbbels in his role as propaganda minister. It appears now that Nazi propaganda was at its most effective when it was reinforcing existing views held by the German public, and rather less so when trying to produce a new value system.

The purpose of Nazi propaganda was to help rid Germany of its old class, religious and ethnic divisions and to help create this sense of national community (*Volksgemeinschaft*). It formed part of the campaign against working class organisations but how effective this was is hard to judge, as many working class members were prepared to accept the benefits of the Nazi handouts whilst still maintaining loyalty to working class associations.

However, there can be no doubt that the youth of Germany enthusiastically embraced the propaganda message and it was this group that the regime targeted to continue the 'Thousand Year Reich'.

Finally, the cult of the leader was a major theme of Nazi propaganda. Hitler was portrayed as being above all party politicking and was portrayed as a figure for national focus and loyalty. This was reinforced by positive achievements of the Hitler regime. Reduction in unemployment and his

foreign policy successes helped to consolidate Hitler's unquestioned position within Germany.

Maintaining a Nazi society – 'The stick'

The police state

In order to ensure the obedience of the people and acceptance of Nazi rule, Hitler and his associates set about creating the apparatus of a police state. Concentration camps were supposed to be 'temporary places of arrest' till opponents of the regime could be 're-educated'. In reality they were to become a feared institution of the state. The regime was able to portray the inmates of these camps as 'enemies' of the state and won the grudging approval of a populace that accepted that most of the inmates were people of whom they disapproved anyway. Certainly, reports at the time indicated that the secret police were eagerly supported by large numbers of people willing to denounce their friends and neighbours. Whether they were or not, the secret police, or *Gestapo*, seemed to be watching and listening everywhere. But the real enforcers of the Nazi state were members of the SS.

Source 11.6

Parade of German SS at a Nazi rally in Nuremberg.

The SS was the state's internal security service, its purpose being to root out any opposition, real or imagined, to the will of the *Führer.* From 1933, it had grown into a powerful, disciplined force, fanatically loyal to Hitler and ably led by Heinrich Himmler. With its distinctive, threatening black uniforms and lightning flash collar symbols, it struck fear into the minds of most Germans. Gordon Craig has concluded that:

> " *The force that prevented the regime from dissolving into chaos was terror and its instrument was the SS.*
>
> Gordon Craig, The Politics of the Prussian Army, *1963*

The failure of Hitler's opponents was due to a combination of factors. They lacked a common aim, leadership and organisation. They failed to realise that only by removing Hitler could the Nazis be overthrown. Too many Germans supported the regime, even if only partly, to ensure any success for its opponents.

Maintain a Nazi society – 'The sweetener'

Nazi foreign policy

Hitler's foreign policy was hugely popular in Germany, especially when he seemed to be reversing the humiliations of Versailles and the Weimar years. His success in the area of foreign policy also stilled the voices of opposition to his regime at home.

Hitler's decision to end all reparations payments was portrayed as a great foreign policy achievement even though this had already been agreed with his Weimar predecessors. In October 1933, Hitler announced Germany's withdrawal from the League of Nations and, more significantly, from the disarmament conference being held in Geneva. In January 1935, as agreed at Versailles, a plebiscite was held in the Saarland to decide if the area should be restored to Germany. The Nazis used every means at their disposal to ensure a 'yes' vote and the result, with 90 per cent supporting a return to the *Reich*, was seen at home as another endorsement of the regime. In the spring of the same year, Hitler announced that Germany would no longer be bound by the military terms of the Treaty of Versailles. The army was to be increased in size. In March 1936, Hitler ordered the remilitarisation of the Rhineland. Now known to be a gamble, the failure of France and Britain to defend its obligations under the Versailles Treaty ensured not only public acclaim for Hitler at home, but also saw his dominance of the army increase.

In *Mein Kampf*, Hitler demanded that the German race be given the living space needed to ensure the survival of the Aryan race. This space, or *Lebensraum*, was to be created from the Slavic lands to the east of Germany and ultimately from Russia. It also had a practical aim – to gain resources available in Russia. With the rearmament of the regime after 1935, Germany needed access to ever more raw materials like coal and oil. Thus Hitler's foreign policy was also motivated by economic needs.

The foreign policy aims of the regime in the second half of the 1930s were made clear by the 'Hossbach Memorandum'. This was a set of notes made after a meeting between Hitler and his generals in November 1937.

Source 11.7

Lands lost at the Treaty of Versailles and lands regained by the Nazis prior to the war.

Legend:
— Germany, 1919
☐ Land lost by Germany at the Treaty of Versailles
▨ Land gained by Germany prior to Second World War

Hitler was reported as saying that the aim of German policy was to make secure and preserve the racial community and to enlarge it. He believed Germany's problem could only be solved by means of force and that was never without risks. Hitler's claim that Germany needed more and more space to expand led to an ever more aggressive and expansionist foreign policy.

Hitler accomplished the *Anschluss* (union) with Austria in March 1938, despite its being forbidden by the Treaty of Versailles and the Treaty of St Germain. The Nazi 'invasion' was endorsed in a plebiscite in April 1938, with 99.75 per cent of Austrians voting in favour of Hitler's actions.

Finally, in September of 1938, Hitler was able to gain the Sudetenland of Czechoslovakia, with its majority of German-speaking citizens. At this point, Hitler had achieved almost complete control over the German people, and he began to believe his own propaganda that he was infallible. The rest of Czechoslovakia was swallowed up in March 1939, again with only criticism but no action from Britain and France. With the Nazi–Soviet Pact of August 1939, Hitler had secured the neutrality of the USSR for his attack upon Poland.

Source 11.8

A Nazi propaganda postcard celebrating the Nazi election victory in the Sudetenland on 4 December 1938. The postcard shows the ethnic German areas of Czechoslovakia, with Czechs welcoming Hitler. The caption reads 'We thank our leader'.

WIR DANKEN UNSERM FÜHRER

Although Hitler's foreign policy successes were portrayed by Göbbels' propaganda machine as evidence of the infallibility of the *Führer*, Hitler was an opportunist. He was skilful in being able to recognise opportunities in foreign affairs – like abandoning the military terms of the Treaty of Versailles in early 1935, to the fury of the French – while negotiating with Britain on a naval agreement, exploiting weaknesses in his opponents and capitalising on events as they arose.

Given this stunning range of foreign policy triumphs, especially in comparison with the years of Weimar failure, it is not surprising that the voices of opposition to the Hitler regime were struggling to be heard. With Germany now recognised as a great power, few were willing to support calls for Hitler's removal from power. As noted by David Welch, 'Much of Hitler's popularity after he came to power rested on his achievements in foreign policy'

Conclusion

Like many aspects of Nazi life, the experiences of different sections of the population varied. For those who supported the Nazis, or just 'went with the flow', life seemed to get better. For those who were against the regime life became more difficult. Nazi racial and foreign policies did bring about fundamental changes in German society, but the so-called 'social revolution' demanded by Röhm and his supporters did not develop during the period of the Third Reich. Hitler's legacy was entirely negative; mass murder, the beginnings of the Cold War and the division of Germany until the last decade of the twentieth century.

Activities

Draw a spider diagram around the central question: 'How did Hitler retain the support of the German people from 1933 to 1939?'

Around your central question, draw at least five boxes. Each box should contain ONE main reason why Hitler remained in power. For example, one of your boxes should contain 'solving Germany's economic problems'. From each of the boxes draw at least three more legs, each one leading to a further development of the reason.

Develop each of the other boxes you have in your diagram. When you have finished you will have the information needed to explain the ways in which Hitler retained popular support between 1933 and 1939.

Sample Essay Questions

1 To what extent did the Nazi regime rely upon fear to maintain power between 1933 and 1939?

2 'A total dictatorship.' To what extent is this an accurate description of the power of the Nazi state in Germany 1933–1939?

Bibliography

Britain & Scotland

Chapter 1

Wright, D.G. *Democracy and Reform 1815–1885*, London: Longman, 1970

Chapter 2

Pugh, M. 'Votes for Women' in *Modern History Review*, Septmeber 1990, Volume 2, No 1

Chapter 5

Barnett, C. *The Audit of War: The Illusion and Reality of Britain as a Great Nation*, London: Pan Books, 2001

Sked, A. and Cook, C. *Post-War Britain: A Political History*, London: Penguin, 1979

Webster, C. *National Health Service: A Political History*, Oxford: Oxford University Press, 2002

www.spartacus.schoolnet.co.uk/ Linsurance1946.htm

Germany

Chapter 6

Carr, W. *A History of Germany*, London: Edward Arnold, 1969

Mitchell, I. *Bismarck and the Development of Germany*, Edinburgh: Holmes McDougall, 1980

Stiles, A. *The Unification of Germany*, London: Hodder and Stoughton, 1990

Thomson, D. *Europe since Napoleon* London: Longman, 1965, quoted in Mitchell, *Bismarck and the Development of Germany*, Edinburgh: Holmes McDougall, 1980

Chapter 7

Thomson, D. *Europe since Napoleon*, London: Longman, 1965

Chapter 8

Feuchtwanger, E. *Bismarck*, London: Routledge, 2002

Mitchell, I. *Bismarck and the Development of Germany*, Edinburgh: Holmes McDougall, 1980

Stiles, A. *The Unification of Germany*, London: Hodder and Stoughton, 1990

Chapter 9

Von Bismarck, O. *Reflections and Reminiscences*, 1898

Cameron, R., Robertson, C. and Henderson, C. *The Growth of Nationalism: Germany and Italy 1815–1939*, Fenwick: Pulse Publications, 1992

Feuchtwanger, E. *Bismarck*, London: Routledge, 2002

Mitchell, I. *Bismarck and the Development of Germany*, Edinburgh: Holmes McDougall, 1980

Seaman, L.C.B. *Vienna to Versailles*, London: Routledge, 1964

Thomson, D. *Europe since Napoleon*, London: Longman, 1965

Chapter 10

Cameron, R., Robertson, C. and Henderson, C. *The Growth of Nationalism: Germany and Italy 1815–1939*, Fenwick: Pulse Publications, 1992

Fulbrook, M. *Hitler*, London: Collins Educational, 2004

Hiden, J. *The Weimar Republic*, London: Longman, 1974

McKichan, F. *Germany 1815–1939*, London: Oliver and Boyd, 1992

Merkl, P. *The Origin of the West German Republic*, Oxford: Oxford University Press, 1963

Nicholls, A.J. *Weimar and the Rise of Hitler*, London: Macmillan, 1970

Simpson, W. *Hitler and Nazi Germany*, Cambridge: Cambridge University Press, 1991

Welch, D. *The Third Reich – Politics and Propaganda 2nd Edition*, London: Routledge, 2002

Chapter 11

Craig, G. *The Politics of the Prussian Army*, Oxford: Oxford University Press, 1963

Fulbrook, M. *Hitler*, London: Collins Educational, 2004

Grunberger, R. *A Social History of the Third Reich*, New York: Holt Rinehart Winston, 1971

McKichan, F. *Germany 1815–1939*, London: Oliver and Boyd, 1992

Simpson, W. *Hitler and Nazi Germany*, Cambridge: Cambridge University Press, 1991

Welch, D. *The Third Reich – Politics and Propaganda 2nd Edition*, London: Routledge, 2002

Index